A Life Inside

A Prisoner's Notebook

Erwin James

Atlantic Books
London

First published in 2003 by Atlantic Books, on behalf of Guardian
Newspapers Ltd. Atlantic Books is an imprint of Grove Atlantic Ltd.

The poem 'Web-Weaving Spider' is reproduced on p.147 by kind permission
of Labhriunn Mac Chalium.

10 9 8 7 6 5 4

A CIP catalogue record for this book is available from
the British Library

ISBN 1 903809 98 3

Printed in Great Britain by Mackays of Chatham Ltd, Chatham, Kent
Design by Helen Ewing

Atlantic Books
An imprint of Grove Atlantic Ltd
Ormond House
26–27 Boswell Street
London WC1N 3JZ

Contents

Foreword

Ian Katz

Erwin James's first *Guardian* column, published in February 2000, was about the arrangements made by a group of prisoners to ensure that as many of them as possible could read a single copy of a newspaper. At first glance, it seemed preoccupied with a fairly obscure detail of prison life. But anyone who read it quickly sensed that a window into another world was opening. In just 800 words, Erwin gave *Guardian* readers a powerful sense of the fragile equilibrium, the complex relationships, the simmering tensions and the paranoia that lie behind Britain's prison walls.

Erwin's particular gift is the ability to tell little, human stories that convey the reality of prison life as powerfully as any weighty monograph or roiling polemic. Over the past three years we have got to know the characters in these stories as well as the lead players of any TV soap: Rinty, the big Dundonian *Antiques Roadshow* fan; Cody, the elderly former sergeant still protesting his innocence after 24 years inside; Felix the Gambler, sometime Buddhist and serial schemer. Though Erwin takes care not to reveal their identities, (all names have been changed and locations obscured), his characters are very real; during one visit he blithely told me that Felix the Gambler had won £28,000 on the horses at Ascot the previous week. Many of his cameo characters are just as memorable. Who will forget the fellow prisoner – promptly christened Torchy – who was admitted to hospital with a number of batteries lodged in his rear end?

'A Life Inside' quickly developed a devoted following among *Guardian* readers. (One letter declaring 'when you're not in the paper I'm devastated' earned a proud spot on Erwin's cell wall.) But Erwin acquired fans in some more surprising places too. On a visit to a lifers-only prison in Portsmouth, the governor told

me that he read the column religiously. At one medium security prison where Erwin was serving, a senior officer begged him
to include him in one of his stories. Martin Narey, Director
General of the prison service, wrote personally to say how much
he admired Erwin's writing. Even the conservative columnist
Barbara Amiel, as improbable an admirer as you could imagine,
wrote praising his 'really compelling and intelligent prose on life
inside'.

One of the reasons Erwin's columns enjoy such wide appeal
is that his writing exhibits no self-pity. The unwritten premise of
the column has always been that he fully accepts the punishment
to which he has been sentenced. But his columns don't peddle
a soft-focus picture of prison life either. Frequently – as when he
described Rinty's recall to prison after being judged to have broken the terms of his life sentence licence, or the moment he
heard that his own minimum term to be served had been
extended from fourteen to twenty-five years, or any of the innu-
merable bureaucratic idiocies in which the prison system spe-
cializes – anger simmers just beneath the surface of his courtly
prose. During visits, his frustration was sometimes more palpable. 'It's hardest when they show you no respect,' he complained
of the particularly officious guards at another medium security
prison where he served. 'Especially when they talk to you like
you're a child.'

Invariably our conversations in the draughty, hangar-like visiting room of that prison (red chairs for prisoners, blue for visitors) turned to the gym. At around six foot two inches tall and
sixteen stone, Erwin cuts an imposing figure – and not by accident. He explained how, on his arrival in prison, he quickly figured out that the best survival strategy was to try to appear
tough. 'You've got to look like you would be too much trouble
to tangle with,' he said. He explained that a key factor in making sure you keep safe on the prison landings is how much you
can bench press. 'If you can manage 100kg you'll be OK in here,'
he told me. He described the hush in the gym when a prisoner
attempted a big lift. When I asked how much he could bench

press, his reply was a little sheepish: 'Er, 150kg.'

Such is the disparity between the burly prison hard-man and the quietly spoken, reflective writer that, on my first visit, I sat at the wrong table for at least ten minutes before concluding that the heavy-set figure sitting alone a few tables away must be the man I was supposed to meet. 'You have to be careful about how much of your real self you reveal in these places if you want to survive,' he said. 'Otherwise you'll be eaten alive, no matter how big and tough you might look.'

During his seventeen years in closed prisons Erwin became a master at the art of survival. By the pathetic standards of prison life, he lived in some comfort. In one memorable column, he describes his unease on being transferred to a so-called 'enhanced wing' with pine bed, in-cell TV and hot and cold running water. What he doesn't mention in the column is that the cell also had a pair of green velvet curtains that he had carried with him from prison to prison. Or that at another prison he had for a time enjoyed the comfort of a large carpet. 'When Ann Widdecombe visited,' he once told me, 'I had to keep my cell door closed so she wouldn't see it.'

Erwin's great achievement was to do much more than simply survive, however. The barely-literate wild man who entered the prison system nineteen years ago will leave it a cultured and intimidatingly well-read graduate with a well-established career as a writer and journalist. During one visit he told me how Jeffrey Archer's *Kane and Abel* was the first book he had read in prison. 'I thought it was great at the time but recently I read it again and I couldn't believe I'd finished it first time around.' As if to complete the circle, Erwin reviewed Archer's prison memoir in the *Guardian*. With deliciously understated contempt he dismissed the more celebrated inmate's approach as 'a lazy, intrusive way to write about prison life'.

Even the most sceptical reader could not say the same about this remarkable collection.

February 2003

Introduction

Erwin James

When I was about sixteen years old I read a newspaper article about a man who had been sentenced to life imprisonment. The report was brief. It gave only the man's name, age and a summary of what he had done. There were no pictures. As I recall, there was nothing sensational in the story. But it had a profound effect on me. Probably because it was the first time I had ever been prompted to think about such an event: somebody going to prison for life. For days afterwards images of the man appeared in my mind. I could see him lying on his bed, or sitting on his chair, perhaps writing a letter home or reading a book, but accompanied night and day by the knowledge of what he had done and thoughts of the long years of incarceration ahead of him. I'm not sure that I felt any sympathy for him, though his situation was undeniably sorrowful. Reading the story made me wonder. What had happened in his life that he should have acted in the way that he did? How did he live with the pain and grief he had caused? And what was it like to have to spend all those years living in a prison cell? I never imagined that some ten years later I would find myself in that very same position.

In fact, it was not until my trial, while I was waiting for the jury's verdict, that I began to think about my life and question how I had become who I was. Reflecting in such a way was a new experience. For as long as I could remember, before then, it seemed that I'd been forever on the move, bowling along from one disaster to another. There had been times when I had tried to live what I thought was a normal life. In spite of the erratic course I had taken, I was a worker and several times had attempted to settle down. But each time I failed, leaving only distress and bad memories in my wake. My trial was the end of the line.

I wanted to be free. That was why I fought the case and pleaded not guilty. But there was no life for me to go back to. There was nobody missing me, or anyone who needed me – at least not the way I was. My rootless, itinerant lifestyle was a freedom of sorts. But when I fantasized about a verdict that would allow me to walk out of the courthouse, I only ever got as far as the pavement. The imagined elation would then turn to despair as I tried to decide which way to turn.

The jury had been sent out late in the morning. As the minutes and hours passed while I sat on the heavy oak bench, or paced the concrete floor, or stood and read the same graffiti over and over on the back wall of the holding cell below the courthouse that they called 'the cage', I began to dread the idea of being free as much as I feared being sent to prison for life. For I knew that life imprisonment was the only sentence the judge could hand down if the verdict went against me.

A lunch of pie, mashed potato and beans was brought to me on a paper plate by a kindly prison officer who looked like he was nearing the end of his career. 'You OK in there?' he asked, after passing the plate through a horizontal gap in the steel gate. I appreciated the warmth in his voice but the last thing I wanted just then was a friendly conversation. His eyes appeared to express compassion. Not for me particularly, but for people in general, I thought. I half smiled and said I was fine. He passed me a polystyrene cup of tea, for which I thanked him, then he nodded and left. I drank the tea, but couldn't face the meal. It remained untouched on the bench for the rest of the afternoon.

When the call came for me to be returned to the courtroom the jury had been out for four hours. I heard the rattling of keys, followed by voices and footsteps, and then the two prison officers who had acted as my escort in court that morning appeared at the gate. 'Ready?' asked the youngest of the pair as he turned the key in the lock. Without answering I pulled on my suit jacket and straightened my tie before stepping outside. The officer locked the gate and, with me in the middle, the three of us set off in single file, striding back along the corridor and up the steep wooden stairs to the court. The door at the top opened directly into the dock. Conversations stopped momentarily and faces turned as the officers and I took our seats. The judge shot a look in my direction and then resumed studying what I assumed were his notes on the case. I stared straight ahead and continued to wait. Several minutes later the door leading to the jury room opened. 'All stand,' called the court usher firmly.

As the jury members filed in quietly, self-consciously, I felt a ball of fire ignite in my stomach. One by one the twelve found their places. The girl with the frizzy blonde hair and bright lipstick; the woman with short black hair who wore an olive coloured blouse; the Asian man with thick eyebrows who wore a black-and-white dog-tooth check jacket; the large stern-faced man in a baggy suit. Even after all this time their faces remain frozen in my mind like a group photograph. When the jury was still the clerk of the court approached the end of the wooden partition and prepared to address the man in the baggy suit. This man looked like someone who had worked hard all his life. His brown hair, flecked with grey, was cut in a severe short back and sides. I guessed he had grown children and grandchildren. A dependable man, I thought. Maybe a retired engineer, or a farmer. Cautious, circumspect, dutiful. An ideal jury foreman.

These were the final moments of my presumed innocence.

'Foreman of the jury,' said the clerk, 'have you reached a verdict upon which you all agree?'

'Yes,' said the foreman.

'Do you find the defendant guilty or not guilty?'

'Guilty.'

Immediately the court became animated. Policemen congratulated each other. Journalists scribbled on their notepads. Lawyers conferred. Observers in the public gallery started chatting, nodding and agreeing. Even the two prison officers with me in the dock relaxed and shared a joke with each other. I just stood there, head bowed, hands by my sides, feeling awkward, embarrassed and ashamed.

A minute or two later the usher brought the court to order

again and my lawyer made a vain attempt to plead some mitigation on my behalf. The judge listened courteously. But there was no room for negotiation. When my lawyer had finished, the judge thanked him and turned to look at me. I stood up straight and held his gaze. He talked briefly about the trial and made condemning comments about my behaviour. In spite of my wretchedness I kept my head up and accepted his words without reaction. Finally the judge said, 'The sentence is mandatory. You will go to prison for life.' Then nodding to the younger officer he added, 'Take him down.'

As I turned my back to the court, my feelings were unambiguous. Whatever my life had been up until the judge sentenced me, whatever it had meant – to me or to anyone else – it was over, and I realised suddenly that I was glad it was over. The relief that I felt as I headed back down the stairs to the cage was unexpected and overwhelming. I had no idea what lay ahead. But it didn't matter. I'd been released from an existence I'd rather not have had in the first place. Regardless of what was to come, I figured it could not be worse than what I had left behind. It took me a long time, though, to recognize that having to spend years in prison might actually be beneficial. It was one thing to be grateful that my destructive way of life had come to an end, but I had never given much thought to how I would manage living in prison. Probably because it was such an awful prospect.

After the trial I was taken to one of the big London prisons where I spent the next year on what is commonly known as '23-hour-bang-up'. The cell door was opened four times a day: three times for meals to be collected, toilet buckets to be emptied and washing water to be collected and once for a walk on the exercise yard – so long as the weather was not 'inclement' (a word I'd never heard before I went to prison). Due to security requirements I was not allowed to use the gym, do any work or use the educational facilities.

For that first year I lived much as I'd imagined the man I'd read about in the newspaper article ten years earlier had lived: reading, exercising and thinking – a lot of thinking. I realized quickly that even though I felt secure for the first time, there was also a frightening precariousness to prison life. The cell doors were opened only briefly at mealtimes, but long enough for the almost daily incidents of violence to take place. The violence appeared to erupt over arguments which had started during the shouting out of cell windows or, more often, it involved ambushes of suspected sex-offenders or attacks on former acquaintances who had turned informer. These 'nonces' and 'grasses', I discovered, were the whipping boys on a prison wing. But violent incidents could also occur spontaneously. Bumping into someone on the landing, catching the eye of someone who didn't appreciate being 'looked at' or simply appearing vulnerable could be enough to unleash the pent-up frustrations that so much bang-up generates.

It was clear that a prisoner's place in the natural order depended on many factors, not least of which was appearance. Looking like you could handle yourself in a fight ensured a generous measure of respect. This was why I embarked on a rigorous in-cell fitness routine of press-ups, sit-ups and running on the spot every day without fail until I was drenched in sweat. Within a few weeks I had established a way of living that was almost ritualized: sleep, eat, read, exercise, wash, eat, read, sleep. I had no idea how long this experience was going to last, but I knew that through it all my first priority was going to be survival.

One day a prison officer arrived at my cell door. He took me down to another cell at the end of the landing that had been converted into a makeshift office. At the door the officer announced, 'Probation' before knocking and allowing me in. The probation officer introduced himself as John and invited me to sit down opposite him. 'I'm doing a report on you,' he said. He had a manila file on his desk with the word 'LIFE' stamped on the front, underneath my name. When he opened it I saw a couple of sheets of typed paper and a card that said, 'Sentence: 99 years.'

'What does that mean?' I said, pointing to the card.

'That's what everybody who is sentenced to life gets,' he said. I was in my mid-twenties at the time and I almost asked him what would happen if I managed to live until I was 124. He looked at me as if he knew what I was thinking and said, 'You'll serve a term in custody. The judge in your trial has recommended that you serve a minimum of fourteen years. When you actually get out after that is entirely up to you. Once you are out you will be on licence for the rest of your life. Which means that you can be recalled to prison at any time and kept in for as long as it is felt desirable by those in authority.'

He said the likelihood was that I'd spend around fifteen or sixteen years in prison, 'depending on how you respond'. He continued, 'Your progress will be monitored throughout. Reports will be prepared every few years by prison staff. Once everyone is agreed that you've changed sufficiently then you'll be let out on licence.' It was odd listening to this man talking about release so soon after my trial. I doubt that he would have understood, however, if I'd tried to explain to him that release was a long way down my list of priorities. I never saw him again, but that man did me a huge service by introducing me to the idea of 'change'. Back in my cell it became the main focus of my thinking. There had to be more to me than what I had become on the outside.

When I started writing for the *Guardian* I had been in prison for nearly sixteen years. During that time I believe I made the changes in my life that I needed to make if I was ever to become a contributing member of society. In some ways, this made being in prison more difficult as it became harder to see it as meaningful. The opportunity to write a regular piece in a newspaper about the reality of life inside came at just the right time and gave me a fresh sense of purpose. But it has to be said that *A Life Inside* is not, and never has been, about me. I mention my trial here and the early months of my imprisonment only as a means of putting the columns into some kind of context. In writing them my only motivation was to try to shed some light on the dark world that is prison. I hope I have achieved that. From the four hours of pacing in the cage below the courthouse, to my present location in 'open conditions' this has been a formidable journey. I'm just thankful that I've made it this far and that I live in a society that is prepared to allow me the privilege of being able to share some of it in this book.

February 2003

Every man, whoever he may be and however low he may have fallen, requires, if only instinctively and unconsciously, respect to be given to his dignity as a human being. The prisoner is aware that he is a prisoner, an outcast and he knows his position in respect to the authorities, but no brands, no fetters, can make him forget that he is a man. And since he is a human being, it follows that he must be treated as a human being. God knows, treatment as a human being may transform into a man again even one in whom the image of God has long been eclipsed.

Fyodor Dostoevsky, 1861

This book is dedicated to
Nancy, Nathalie, Nicki, Victoria,
and all the volunteers, for their work
at the Prisoners' Advice Service.

Closed conditions

How Beggsy fell out with Bob

It was only a tiff, but it could easily have escalated into something much more serious. Let me explain. In this prison we live on 'spurs': dark, warren-like corridors, flanked on either side by a row of cells. On a spur, there are twelve single cells and one double. There are usually two spurs to a landing. The occupants are serving terms of anything from a couple of years to life. Not surprisingly, with so many men forced to live together in such close proximity for such long periods of time, tensions can sometimes run high.

Each day a newspaper is issued to the spur by the prison officer designated to the landing, and each cell takes it in turn to have that day's paper first. Spur etiquette requires the first recipient of the paper to pass it on to his neighbours once he's read it. And herein lies our problem.

Since the papers are issued at lunchtime, the man who is 'on the paper' is expected to read it over the lunchtime bang-up. (Any period a prisoner spends locked in his cell is known as 'bang-up', and the lunchtime period lasts for at least an hour and a half.) He then passes it on to his neighbour, who reads it during the teatime bang-up (at least an hour) before passing it to his neighbour in time for the night-time bang-up, which begins at eight.

But it doesn't stop there.

As soon as the prison officers working the day shift hand in their keys, a relatively small crew takes over for the night. Thereafter, the night patrolman can be heard padding ghost-like along the deserted corridors at hourly intervals. On entering the spur during his nine o'clock visit, the 'night cocky', as he is affectionately known, will notice a newspaper protruding from beneath one of the locked cell doors. On closer inspection he will find a message scrawled across the top of the paper, 'Guv, please pass to number four. Cheers!'

For perhaps obvious reasons, night cockies do not carry cell-door keys, so our kind helper will bend down and carefully slide the paper under the appointed door. Finally, on his ten o'clock trip, he will transfer the paper to cell number five by the same method. In this way, if all goes smoothly, each day at least five spur residents will get to read that day's paper. Unfortunately, however, one night last week it all went pear-shaped.

Joe was on the paper first and passed it to Eddy, who read it at teatime. That night it was supposed to be Bob's turn at eight, Johnny Beggs's at nine, and Duwayne's at ten. The problem arose when Bob took his turn at eight, read the paper, and then promptly fell asleep. Duwayne is so laid-back that as far as he was concerned it was no big deal. But Beggsy, from London's East End, took it badly. Worse than that, he took it personally.

Bob knew he had done wrong and the next morning, as soon as the cell doors were unlocked at ten past eight, he went straight to Beggsy's cell and tapped gently on his door.

'Who is it?' called Beggsy from underneath the bedcovers.

'It's Bob,' said Bob, almost whispering. 'I've got the paper for you.'

After a momentary silence, Beggsy responded. 'Go stick the fackin' paper up your fackin' arse you caant!' he yelled, giving Bob no chance to apologize.

For the next few days there was a heavy atmosphere on the spur as the two men insisted on blanking each other. It got worse as they began bad-mouthing one another behind each other's back, and soon two camps had emerged. Things were looking ominous until this week, when Beggsy got his transfer to the 'enhanced' wing, the Shangri-La of prison accommodation, where residents have pine beds and in-cell television.

'Have you heard about that snake then?' asked Bob, soon after I had returned from morning labour.

'Who?' I said, feigning ignorance.

'That bastard Beggs,' he said heatedly. 'He's off to the enhanced wing tomorrow.'

'Oh yeah?' I said.

'Yeah,' he replied. 'I wonder how many names he's put up to get over there.'

I picked up my dinner plate and said nothing.

'Everybody knows they're all grasses and wrong 'uns on that wing,' he continued. 'Or the governor's blue-eyed boys.'

Later, I heard a whisper that Bob had been overheard quietly asking the landing officer (ahem) where *his* name was on the waiting list for transfers to the enhanced wing. Blatant and brass-necked, it won't be long before he's wheeling his trolley across the yard too. And don't worry, there's no danger of a confrontation when Bob lands on the comfy wing. Trust me − in a few weeks' time we'll see him and Beggsy walking around the exercise yard giving an award-winning performance of the old pals' act. You'd have to live in these places to understand. But all they really needed was a bit of space.

17 February 2000

Barrier methods

Conjugal visits are unavailable to prisoners in British jails − officially that is. But the revelation last week that, despite separation by a barred gate, a couple locked in adjacent cells below Swansea Crown Court had managed to enjoy a sexual encounter while the guards weren't looking shows that you can lock people up, but you can't stop them doing what comes naturally if the opportunity arises.

Having said that, as far as sex is concerned a monk-like existence is the best that most male prisoners can hope for. Of course, it takes a strong will and a disciplined mind to withstand the demands of the primal urge for any significant length of time. Long hours spent in confinement without the succour of human warmth serve only to intensify the sense of carnal deprivation. The landings of long-term prisons are littered with wan individuals, hollow-eyed through years of unrestrained masturbation. Pathetic perhaps, but for those unable to master their instincts there are few options available through which to gain relief from the torment of Priapus.

Some are reduced to desperate measures. One man I knew of some years ago found himself in an extremely embarrassing situation, as well as a painful one, after apparently attempting to achieve some pleasure from performing an act upon himself involving four RS20 batteries, taped together lengthways. The man ended up being rushed to an outside hospital when the tape came apart and two of the batteries were left lodged deep inside his rectum. When news of his 'accident' reached the wings, ruthless jail wags christened him Torchy, and the name stuck for the remainder of his sentence.

The 'married quarters' is the section of a wing or landing where men who prefer to adopt a gay lifestyle (albeit in private) tend to congregate. The need for physical intimacy can be so great that inhibitions and taboos may be cast aside for the palliative effect of warm skin upon warm skin, and not all who locate themselves within this community are full-time homosexuals; some are 'jail gays' only and may well have wives or girlfriends who visit regularly, unaware of their imprisoned partner's complex coping strategy.

Before the introduction of CCTV, visiting-room sex also used to cause major headaches for the authorities. While most couples managed to confine their intimacies to discreet fumblings under tables, others were not so inhibited. I remember once in the visiting room of a maximum security prison a woman was sitting blatantly astride the man she was visiting, chatting and laughing and gently moving her hips backwards and forwards. Though nothing could be seen beneath her long dress, it did not take a great deal of imagination to work out what was going on. As usual, at the end of visiting time the prisoners formed an orderly queue at one end of the room while the visitors lined up at the other end, by the exit. Everyone was waiting in silence for the two groups to be counted – everyone except the amorous couple, who by then had become vigorously animated in their endeavour to achieve satisfaction.

It was a surreal scene made even more absurd when, once

they'd finished, the woman simply climbed off her partner, straightened her dress and walked briskly across the room to join the other visitors. The man stood up, adjusted his denims and then sauntered over to tag on to the end of the prisoners' queue. 'All complete!' shouted the officer monitoring the prisoners. 'Thank you, sir!' came the reply from his colleague standing by the visitors.

As soon as the control room had been informed by radio that everyone in the visiting room had been accounted for, the two groups vacated the premises in the usual way, as if nothing untoward had taken place.

Exhibitions like that are rare nowadays, what with more hi-tech surveillance, and robust floor patrols. But the tensions generated by forced celibacy continue.

Sadly, and perhaps surprisingly in view of the current social climate, the issue of how prisoners are meant to manage their sexual needs while incarcerated, and later upon release, remains unacknowledged by the authorities. An associate of mine, recently released after eighteen years inside, was so concerned about the prospect of renewed sexual relations that shortly before his day of liberation he decided to broach the subject with the prison psychologist, who happened to be female.

'What should I expect with regard to my first sexual experience?' he asked sheepishly.

'What do you mean?' replied the psychologist.

'Is there anything I should be aware of that might or, er… might not happen?' he elaborated, even more sheepishly.

The psychologist was dismissive in her response, and not a little embarrassed. She quickly ushered my confused acquaintance out of the office. As he told me later, 'If I'd wanted to speak about sexual deviancy, we'd probably have been talking all week.'

Sexual interaction between human beings is a precious and potent gift. As the couple in Swansea demonstrated beautifully, steel bars may take away our liberty, but sexual desire cannot be so easily contained.

25 February 2000

Hoping today for jam tomorrow

'He's living in false hope,' say the prison sceptics, usually in reference to some likely lad who has applied for parole but has failed to deal with his 'offending behaviour'. But is there really such a thing as false hope?

At six foot one and more than fifteen stone, Stubbsy is a big man. On a good day he can be fun, endearing even, in an adolescent sort of way. Unfortunately for his neighbours on the spur, however, good days are rare.

He likes to brag that he was once an international kick-boxing champion, though apart from juvenile kung-fu-type demonstrations in the queue at mealtimes he never produces any evidence. Likewise when he recounts the tale of his 'epic scrap in Strangeways', which, according to Stubbsy, resulted in the death of his opponent. 'I opened him right up,' he snarls in his throaty Mancunian accent, illustrating with a thrust and a grimace, 'but there were no witnesses see, so I got away with it.'

In reality, however, there are very few genuine tough guys in prison. Most are just ordinary men with extraordinary failings, and at heart everybody knows it. But don't be fooled by the 'holiday camp' theorists – prison is a scary place and a strategy for survival is essential.

The problem for men like Stubbsy, who choose to cultivate a fierce reputation, is that the more outrageous the claims, the more likely they are to attract unwelcome attention. 'Big mouths hide big secrets,' say the old hands.

Soon 'cuttings merchants' will be consulted (men who wield power by collecting newspaper cuttings of reported crimes, sometimes going back years) or letters will be written to friends in other jails. Whatever secrets are being guarded will not be secret for long. And so it was for Stubbsy.

Within weeks of him landing, the 'facts' were out and the grapevine was humming. The latest gag relating to the big man goes something like this:

'What's Stubbsy's favourite chat-up line?'

'I don't know, what is it?'

'Scream and I'll kill you.'

Stubbsy hasn't heard it yet, but he will. At the moment he's preoccupied with what the wags are calling his 'get-out-of-jail-free card'. According to how he tells it, he awoke one night in another jail to find his cellmate hanging from the bars of the window. The man apparently survived after Stubbsy cut him down. Later, someone suggested that he might get a pardon for his actions. Stubbsy wrote to the Home Office, who sent him a card upon which was scribbled, 'Dear Mr Stubbs, your enquiry is being considered.'

'I saved the guy's life,' he insists, brandishing the card under uninterested noses. 'Surely that makes jam worth hoping for?' (Jam roll = parole.) 'Sure Stubbsy,' is the usual reply, while knowing looks are exchanged behind his back.

Krebbe is another one looking for a shortcut out. A middle-aged recidivist, he's decided that he's had enough. A couple of weeks ago he volunteered to 'two-up' in the double cell with Little Joe. Horrific childhood sexual abuse has left Little Joe deeply troubled, and his self-loathing regularly manifests itself in self-inflicted wounds to arms, legs, neck and face. Recently he has taken to inserting objects into his body: a pencil in an arm, matchsticks in his ankles. He's been out to the local hospital so often that the senior consultant has finally said: no more. Krebbe smelled Brownie points. 'I'll keep an eye on him,' he told the wing governor. 'All he needs is someone to listen.'

For a while the arrangement went well. Krebbe regained some cred. He seemed to be succeeding where everyone else had failed – until the other night. Little Joe was sitting on the toilet behind the modesty curtain when Krebbe noticed droplets of blood spattering by his protruding feet. 'What's happening?' Krebbe shouted, yanking back the curtain.

Joe was busy reopening a deep crevice in his forearm with a craft knife. He glared at Krebbe and then leapt at the older man, catching him across the stomach with the bloody blade. 'It was like the shower scene from *Psycho*,' Krebbe later recounted. After putting Joe in an arm-lock he alerted the prison officers by pressing the cell's alarm button. The next day it was all he could talk about. 'I'm putting the bastard right in,' he ranted in the television room. 'I've made a statement. This is going to get me out!'

He quietened down the day after when the potential repercussions of his spouting off dawned on him. Being labelled a grass can have worse consequences in jail than being called a 'nonce' (sex offender). But Krebbe will not be deterred from hoping for an early release. Like Stubbsy, the more he dwells on the possibility, the more he will become convinced of the certainty. False hope? No, only hope.

2 March 2000

The rage of the innocent

It must be difficult to be in prison if you are innocent. That's not to say it's easy if you're guilty, but at least if you are you can take comfort from the knowledge that the system is geared to accommodate you. For the guilty, trained people wait ready and eager to help with the 'coming to terms' process. A 'sentence plan' will identify 'risk factors' to be addressed and determine the most appropriate 'offending-behaviour' programmes to be attended (anger management or victim empathy, for example).

Once targets have been set, review boards sit periodically to make recommendations based on each prisoner's progress. Depending on the prisoner's response to the sentence, it may be possible to win an earlier release. But what if the prisoner is innocent? How does he begin to 'come to terms' with his situation? How does he address his 'offending behaviour'? And, no less important, how does he cope with the vagaries of daily life in a hostile environment knowing he's not supposed to be there?

I thought about these questions several days ago when I

bumped into Cody as he was coming out of the main kitchen at the end of morning labour. As he raised his arms for the prison officer carrying out the routine rub-down search, our eyes met and he smiled.

'She's 'ad it!' he called to me, adding with a loud cackle over the officer's shoulder, 'A little girl.'

'Congratulations,' I called back, returning his smile. 'When?'

'Last night,' he said. 'They came and told me through the cell door. So that sorts that problem out.'

The problem Cody was talking about concerned a much-anticipated visit from a daughter expecting his latest grandchild. Visits may be booked by phone up to six weeks in advance, and visitors must present proof of identity on arrival. A recently introduced child-protection measure also stipulates that, as with adults, the names of all visitors under eighteen and details of their relationship to the prisoner must be included on the visiting order (VO). The date Cody requested for his daughter's visit was two weeks after the day on which she was expecting to give birth.

'Any children coming?' asked the prison officer dealing with Cody's VO application.

'Yes, one baby,' said Cody.

'Relationship?'

'Grandchild.'

'Name?'

'I don't know yet.'

The officer slowly looked up from his desk.

'What? You don't know your own grandchild's name?'

'Er, no,' said Cody. 'It's not been born yet.'

'Well, I'm sorry,' insisted the officer, 'the rules say I've got to have a name.'

'But I've told you,' said Cody, raising his voice. 'It ain't been *bawn* yet!'

Fortunately good sense prevailed on both sides and eventually a compromise was agreed upon. The VO would be issued and the baby's name was to be added as soon as the birth had taken place. How much easier life would be for Cody if only all his problems could be resolved so amicably.

Last year he applied for 'enhanced' status. (Under the 'incentives and earned privileges scheme', or IEPS, currently in operation throughout the prison system, prisoners have access to three lifestyle regimes: 'basic', 'standard', and 'enhanced'.) A week or so after his application Cody was called to the wing office.

'We have to refuse your application,' said the wing governor.

'Why's that?' said Cody.

'You're still in denial.'

'But I'm innocent,' said Cody.

'I'm sorry,' said the governor, 'those are the rules.'

Since Cody is doing life and has been protesting his innocence for more than twenty years, this obstacle seemed insurmountable. This year, however, the rules changed. So long as the prisoner is being cooperative, being 'in denial' will not count against him. Cody reapplied for enhanced status. But before the application could be processed an incident occurred.

Cody was walking around the exercise yard alone. With the collar of his heavy prison jacket turned up, and his grey hair, specs and slight stoop, he must have looked like a vulnerable target to the unknowing. He heard the sound of someone spitting and felt something land on his back moments before two young men in PE gear jogged past him laughing. No way could the old man have stood for such an insult. He watched from the corner of his eye as the joggers completed another circuit of the yard. This time when they approached, Cody turned and whipped off his jacket. For a sixty-seven-year-old he gave a good account of himself. He managed to rub the spit in the face of the biggest of the two joggers and stayed upright as blows were exchanged.

Luckily the fight was stopped by prison staff before any real damage could be inflicted on the joggers, but later Cody had another surprise in store. Back on the wing he was called to the office once again.

'I'm sorry,' the governor told him, 'but we cannot grant you your enhanced yet.'

'But I thought "in denial" couldn't count against me now,' said Cody.

'It doesn't,' replied the governor. 'But you've been fighting. That's not what we expect of enhanced prisoners.'

Now I don't know for sure if Cody is innocent. But if he is, you have to agree, it surely must be difficult.

16 March 2000

How Grady crashed on the fast track out

They came and took Grady away last week. Without ceremony, the three prison officers from the security department (also responsible for cell searches and endearingly known as 'burglars') marched him out of the wing and across the crowded exercise yard en route to the segregation block. But there were no calls of protest from his fellow cons, as might have been expected in such a situation, no cries of support for a comrade. Just silence, and a host of baleful glances in the wretched man's direction.

A graduate of a jail with a ground-breaking 'therapeutic regime' (a regime that includes daily prisoner-led group psychotherapy sessions), Grady should have been on the fast track through the system. His crime was serious, but by no means major league for a lifer. After his successful stint in the therapeutic jail, rehabilitation and reintegration into the outside community at the earliest opportunity should have been little more than a formality. There was only one obstacle: a year or so in a mainstream prison – his test period – before being considered for a downgrade to Category D status and a transfer to 'open conditions'. All he had to do was to 'keep his head down', as they say.

But within days of his arrival here he was approached by a prison officer and asked if he would like to join the fledgling prison 'listener scheme'. ('Listeners' are prisoners trained by the Samaritans to support their fellows through times of crisis.) 'We think you have the right qualities,' the officer told him.

13

Prisoners are often suspicious of new arrivals and especially wary of those who appear to want to set themselves apart from their peers. Perhaps a wiser man would have taken more time to answer. Much better to settle in first and gain a little trust from the neighbours before getting involved in 'community initiatives'. But Grady was too eager, too keen to make a good impression. 'I've done a lot of therapy,' he told the officer. 'I think I know what makes these lads tick.'

Soon he made the acquaintance of a man called Boots. Though not a big man, Boots's position in the prison hierarchy was well established, mainly thanks to his disposition towards spontaneous violence – kicking heads in was a speciality. Boots was impressed by the charismatic newcomer and quickly began to defend him against a burgeoning band of critics, who were suspicious of the time Grady appeared to spend in the wing office, allegedly 'on listener business'.

'He's a screw's man,' they said.

'No,' said Boots.

'He's a grass!'

'No!'

But ill-feeling towards Grady was becoming frenzied, fired by the perception that he considered himself to be in some way superior to everyone else on the wing.

'Jug him!' said one man (meaning to scald him with a jug or two of boiling water from the urn, mixed with sugar so it would stick).

'Cut him!' said another. (The favoured weapon is razor blades melted into the end of a toothbrush.)

It was strange, though, to witness the reaction when Grady's cell was burnt out while he was at work. (Lighted rags were scattered over bedding and furniture, clothes ruined, photographs destroyed.) Much kudos awaited the perpetrator. Yet nobody claimed responsibility. Very strange. But, in a way, the arsonist had done Grady a favour. He was moved immediately to D Wing where his troubles should have been over.

Instead, Bruce the Aussie – a man known by several long-termers to have served a previous sentence for a sex offence but whose secret had yet to be revealed – decided that continuing the campaign against his new neighbour could be a useful way of deflecting unwanted attention.

'There's an informer on the spur, lads!' he proclaimed, pointing towards the cell where Grady was installing his few intact possessions.

'Sssssss,' came the reply in chorus. (An informer in prison is known as a 'grass' from the phrase 'snake in the grass'.)

Each day thereafter, backwards and forwards to his cell, Grady walked the gauntlet. There were further incidents: a gallon of detergent splattered over his bed; excrement wrapped in a newspaper left under his pillow. He endured it all in silence – until the day he received the answer to his latest review from the Home Office. 'Not suitable for open conditions. Further testing required in closed conditions.'

Of course the official version would be different but, according to the word in the exercise yard, it was then that Grady turned. There had been whispers for a while that Bruce the Aussie was secretly attending the SOTP (sex offender treatment programme) and they say that Grady decided to find out if it was true.

If his plan was to expose Bruce as a nonce he stood little chance against such a skilled manipulator. When the Aussie got wind that Grady was on his case, he made an official complaint to the effect that Grady was trying to hinder his 'rehabilitative efforts' and in the process subvert the much-lauded SOTP. The next day Grady was lifted.

The story of Grady's downfall has been told and retold to much chortling and thigh-slapping in the past few days. Only one man has been conspicuously silent. His name? I'm not saying. Just that he has a fondness for steel toe-caps – and lighted rags.

30 March 2000

Rigging the viewing figures

Big Rinty 'fae Dundee' looked perplexed. He was scrutinizing the television listings guide pinned up each day on the wing noticeboard. 'Look!' he exclaimed, thrusting a tobacco-stained finger aggressively at the adjacent voting sheet on which wing residents can indicate in pencil their preferred choice for the evening's viewing. 'The damned cartel's done it again!'

Understandably, television in prison remains a matter of some contention for many on the outside. The idea that convicts are just lying back and soaking up the soaps when they're supposed to be paying their debt to society is not a very palatable one. But, like most popular perceptions of prison life, the truth is hardly so simple.

Years ago, for example, everybody had to watch what the toughest man in the room wanted to watch. Televised events of world importance occasionally inspired an officially authorized free vote, but even then there was no guarantee that the historic moment would be witnessed. Apparently, when Neil Armstrong's first steps on the moon were due to be repeated one evening in 1969, a kindly prison officer on one wing of a bleak southern jail, infamous for its moorland location, asked for a show of hands.

'We've only got the one telly, lads,' he is reported to have said, smiling apologetically at the men staring at the flickering black-and-white screen from their hard wooden benches, 'so we're going to have a vote.'

There were two choices: the lunar landing, or *Steptoe and Son*. Nobody who has ever served time in a British prison would be in the slightest bit surprised to learn that *Steptoe and Son* won the vote hands down – or rather, hands up.

Wisely, in later years prisons provided two television rooms per wing, one showing BBC and the other showing ITV. But while this measure allowed for more choice (and, with easy chairs, more comfort) it did little to eliminate other causes of conflict, most notably seat reservation.

Since in-cell television is still far from a universal privilege, seat reservation in communal TV rooms continues in many jails. Where it persists, woe betide the freshly arrived ingénue who dares to sit down without first asking others present, 'Excuse me, is this anyone's seat?' For ignorance is no defence. If he's lucky the chair will 'belong' to a confident chap, in for a 'respectable crime' such as armed robbery or GBH. This type of prisoner has nothing to prove and, so long as the chair is vacated rapidly at the first signal of his approach, the odds are that no harm will result.

The danger lies in the possibility that the chair belongs to someone with a dubious history and of scant stature – someone like Binbags for instance (so christened after being caught during a strip-search wearing a plastic bin liner between his Baby-Oil-covered torso and his clothing).

Years earlier, in a high-security prison, Binbags had arrived for his regular mid-week fix of *EastEnders* only to discover his seat had been taken by a new prisoner. He knew he could not afford to lose the potential confrontation and so took what he believed to be the only appropriate action in the circumstances. Without a word he exited quickly, but returned minutes later carrying a jug of boiling water. In the dark, malodorous room, a couple of dozen pairs of eyes watched in silence as Binbags crept up behind the newcomer.

The screams emitted as the hot liquid cascaded down the back of the innocent's neck temporarily drowned out the Albert Square drama's signature tune. But as soon as the jugging victim had fled the room in agony and terror and Binbags had reclaimed his seat, everyone settled down and enjoyed a pleasant, interruption-free half-hour's entertainment.

In a medium-security prison like this one, such incidents are less frequent. But questionable activities such as programme-choice vote-rigging have been winding Rinty up of late, and Felix the Gambler is in the frame. One of our TV rooms is reserved for the showing of films taped from the satellite movie channels. What gets shown in the other room depends on the vote. For shows like *The Bill*, *Bad Girls* and *Crimewatch* there's never any dispute. But Rinty's favourite programme is *Antiques Roadshow*, and Felix's cartel keeps voting for the other side: *Star Trek: The Next Generation*.

'Ah canny watch that shite,' said Rinty through gritted teeth, adding ominously, 'I'm going to sort this out tonight.'

I'd hoped that any trouble would be over by the time I got to the TV room that evening. But when I opened the door and stepped inside I was shocked by what I found. There at the front of the darkened, half-empty room, sat Rinty, listening intently as Hugh Scully waxed lyrical.

'What happened?' I whispered to the man in the next seat as I sat down quietly. 'Where's the cartel?'

'They're all next door watching the movie,' he whispered back.

The previous week Rinty had been learning 'conflict resolution' on the 'enhanced thinking skills' course, and clearly some of it had sunk in. I found out later that he had persuaded George the video orderly to show the sci-fi thriller *Armageddon*, a treat Felix and his cartel of Trekkies could not resist.

There's a rumour that George demanded a fee for the favour. But everyone's agreed – it was worth a phonecard to avoid an unscheduled episode of *Casualty*.

13 April 2000

'I'll smash your doll's house to bits'

Standing in the breakfast queue the other morning, I was suddenly reminded of how easy it is to make the worst of enemies in prison. Several places ahead of me, I thought I saw the hind form of a character I believed I'd left behind for good a long time ago. Small, hunched, balding: surely not... 'Shortly!' I whispered. And the memories came flooding back.

Some years ago, in a quiet northern jail, a middle-aged lifer named Shortly Malone worked alongside Old Ted, an affable, silver-haired man in his sixties who was serving twenty years. The two men worked unsupervised in a converted storeroom, building doll's houses from scrap wood, which, when sold, raised funds for good causes. Both 'red-bands' (trusted prisoners who wear a red armband to indicate their status), they hoped to progress to a less secure prison on the strength of their good conduct and charity work.

Then Saleem arrived, also serving life. He had a brother on the outside who, along with his family, faced eviction for rent arrears. Saleem asked the prison governor if 'for the sake of the children' a loan could be arranged from the charity fund to help his brother. Sensing an opportunity to promote race relations in the prison, the governor asked Shortly and Ted to build a 'special' doll's house. 'When it's finished we'll hold an auction for it,' he enthused, 'and the proceeds can go towards alleviating Saleem's brother's plight.'

Shortly, however, was outraged. 'It's all fookin' wrong,' he protested to Ted. 'We're not here to work for that lot.'

'Get on with you man,' said Ted. 'It's just a job like all the rest.'

But Shortly would not be persuaded. 'If you try and build that doll's house,' he threatened, 'I'll smash it to fookin' bits.'

Ted's hands were tied, so he decided to explain the problem to the governor. 'OK. Not to worry,' said the governor. 'The solution is simple. I'll set Saleem to work alongside you both, and then he can build his own doll's house.' When Shortly heard of the new development he was incandescent. 'Bastard!' he ranted. But then he came up with his own solution.

It was a simple plan. He was going to slip illegal drugs into Saleem's tea and then put an anonymous letter addressed to the staff into the wing postbox. If all went smoothly, when the innocent man's subsequent drug test proved positive, he would be sacked instantly, and might even get a week or two in the punishment block. 'And don't you go saying owt,' he warned Ted.

Ted was appalled. Recognizing the possibility of a major injustice occurring, he ignored Shortly's threats and reported his diminutive workmate's plotting to the governor, who promptly closed down the workshop. Several weeks later, after Shortly had taken a job elsewhere in the prison, the workshop was reopened and Ted and Saleem were reinstated. Shortly kept his distance from the two men, but secretly harboured a grudge against Ted.

Some months earlier Shortly had married a woman he'd met whilst in prison through the columns of a lonely hearts magazine. She lived in London but drove north every two weeks to visit her husband in jail. In the visitors' waiting room one day, Mrs Shortly struck up a conversation with a pretty young woman who had also travelled from London to visit her boyfriend.

'I always come by train,' said the young woman. 'But it's so expensive.'

The older woman appeared sympathetic. 'Why don't I give you a lift?' she suggested. They talked for a while and then an arrangement was agreed upon. Every two weeks from then on, the two women travelled north together.

Naturally their conversations revolved around the men they were visiting. Eventually, the older woman began to speak of how her husband was 'under pressure from an old guy he once worked with'. Her husband was 'vulnerable and shouldn't be locked up with all those criminals', she protested.

Then one day on the way to the jail she stopped the car near a postbox. 'Would you post this for me,' she said, handing the young woman a sealed envelope. The young woman did as she was asked and then climbed back into the car.

'That'll teach that old bugger Ted,' said the older woman as she turned the car into the traffic. 'That was an anonymous letter to the Home Office telling them he's planning an escape.'

Revenge would be sweet, the conspiring couple must have thought, no doubt expecting Ted to be moved to maximum security. How fortunate then that the young woman revealed the plot to her boyfriend, a young man who, though in prison, was not totally bereft of a sense of moral responsibility. After the visit the young man told all to the governor.

'Sit tight,' the governor instructed Ted. 'When the letter arrives, we'll act.'

Weeks passed, but the letter did eventually arrive (after passing through several Home Office departments) and, true to his word, the governor had Shortly transferred to maximum security.

Ted has since been released and now lives quietly in the West Country. Saleem is in an open prison awaiting the outcome of his latest parole review. The whereabouts of Shortly are unknown at the present time, but I can't help feeling a not inconsiderable measure of relief that it wasn't that little conspirator in the breakfast queue the other morning.

27 April 2000

The story of an innocent man

I heard Ricky Vance before I saw him. He was strumming his guitar and singing alone in the prison's 'multi-faith' room as I was walking past on my way to the exercise yard one Saturday afternoon late last year. Intrigued, I stopped by the opaque glass-panelled door and listened. 'I'll be free/one day you'll see/you don't know me/oh baby, don't lie/come on and rescue me…' The lyrics were simple but powerfully delivered as he strained his vocal cords with a passion reminiscent of a grunge musician unplugged. Suddenly the music stopped. Before I could step back and continue on my way the door swung open, making me jump.

'Hi!' he said, smiling. His fair hair was cut short at the back and sides and his eyes were as blue as cobalt.

'Er, hi,' I replied, a little guiltily. I felt as if I'd been caught eavesdropping on a private conversation. 'I was just passing when I heard the music.'

'I could see you through the glass,' he said. 'What did you think?'

'It was good,' I responded. 'You've got talent. What the hell are you doing in prison?'

The question was not meant to be taken literally. It was just supposed to be a compliment, but his response made me wish I hadn't asked it.

'I shouldn't even be in here,' he said, his face darkening instantly. 'I'm innocent.'

It was the perfect conversation stopper.

He asked me if I'd like to go into the room and listen some more. The song he'd been singing was one he'd composed himself and he had others he'd like me to listen to. 'I'd really appreciate your opinion,' he said, his face bright with enthusiasm once more.

'I'm sorry, but there's someone waiting for me out in the yard,' I said, retreating. 'Another time maybe.'

As I walked away I felt another twinge of guilt. I was in no hurry. There was nobody waiting for me. But the young man's manner was unsettling, and I wasn't in the mood to listen to another 'I've been framed' story.

A few days later I was walking around the exercise yard with Stu (due to his wise counsel, also known in here as the Guru) and the young musician was jogging alone.

'Who is that kid?' I said to Stu as he passed us by.

'That's Ricky Vance,' he said. 'On the out he was a singer with a promising career ahead of him apparently – until he was convicted of rape. Now he is doing five years.'

'Christ,' I said.

I'd never heard of Ricky before, but Stu told me that his case had been high profile. 'It was in all the papers,' he said. 'That's why he gets so much grief.'

Over the following weeks I became acutely aware of the grief directed at Ricky Vance. Sometimes it was verbal, and sometimes it was physical, particularly from a little crew of 'plastics' (wannabe gangsters) led by a man called Moser. But Ricky stood his ground and refused to go 'on the rule' (rule 45: segregation for one's own protection).

Eventually he latched on to the Guru, who asked me if I'd help Ricky to write a letter to his MP requesting support. 'The guy's really struggling,' he said.

A couple of days later Ricky turned up at my cell door with several sheets of spidery longhand. I was struck by the sincere tone. 'But you'll have to take out all the references to God,' I advised. He left an hour or so later, seemingly pleased with my efforts.

The next time I saw him was in the hospital wing where I was working temporarily as the orderly. He'd been brought in after having been ambushed by Moser and his gang wielding large batteries in socks. Tears were streaming down his bruised and bloody face.

'Why... won't... they... listen?' he sobbed. I had no answer.

That night he was shipped out to another jail and no more was heard of him until the other week when I picked up one of the wing newspapers. The headline on page three caught my eye, 'Rape-case man cleared'.

Sure enough it was Ricky Vance, exonerated by the Court of Appeal. In the piece he recounted the violent assaults he'd suffered whilst inside and said that he'd often feared for his life. 'Christ,' I whispered.

Word spread quickly and the next day Big Rinty confronted Moser in the exercise yard. 'I hope you're ashamed now of the way you treated that boy,' he said, loud enough for all to hear.

The yard went quiet and still.

'Not really,' said Moser, looking around uneasily. 'He deserved it anyway, for being so arrogant.'

'Well maybe he had a right to be,' said Rinty.

Moser turned and walked away. The yard moved on.

11 May 2000

When a man's got to go... he can't

Without warning, as I was sitting quietly drinking a cup of tea and listening to the news on the radio one day last week, the flap covering the observation panel on my cell door was lifted.

'Are you in there?' said an authoritative voice. I was waiting for the call to morning labour and since the owner of the voice was staring directly into my eyes, the question seemed superfluous.

'Er, yes guv,' I said. From my side of the door, the horizontal perspex panel looked like the eye section of a police photo-fit kit.

'Good,' said the voice, as the flap slammed down and the cell door flew open. ''Cos there's a man here who has come to take the piss out of you.'

The man speaking was not our regular landing officer. Nevertheless his manner was jocular and reassuring in a way. He didn't mean me any harm. His 'joke' was just a way of trying to lighten what he knew was going to be a dignity-reducing exercise for all concerned. Standing next to him was an officer dressed in black combat fatigues: the uniform of 'the burglars'.

As the man in black pulled a plastic folder from under his arm, its logo, printed in large capital letters, registered immediately: MDT. He was collecting candidates for the mandatory drug testing unit.

'Aha,' I said, 'a piss test.'

'Would you mind accompanying this officer?' said the first officer. I pulled on my denim jacket and walked out on to the spur, closing the cell door behind me.

'Sure,' I said.

The MDT officer motioned me to follow him. And then I remembered – I'd only just 'been' five minutes or so before his arrival.

Three hard-backed chairs formed the waiting area outside the room where the samples were taken. I followed the officer through the unmarked door into the (appropriately perhaps) yellow-lit room, which looked like a small office but for the waist-high brick stall in the far corner. Angled on the ceiling directly above the stall, a convex mirror betrayed the presence of a toilet bowl.

'Sit down please,' said the officer. He explained that there were four possible reasons for such a summons: random selection; risk assessment; reasonable suspicion; or voluntary frequent-test programme. 'You've been randomly selected by the computer,' he said. At least it was good to know that I wasn't there as a result of a 'note in the box'. I signed all the copies of the explanatory form and then handed the officer back his pen. 'Ready yet?' he asked.

'No,' I replied, deciding against an explanation.

'OK,' he said, nodding towards the washbasin this side of the modesty stall. 'Take a glass of water and wait outside. You've got four hours.'

In the waiting area two new arrivals with close-cropped hair, stained T-shirts and scuffed trainers were engaged in ribald conversation. I sat down and began willing the water to pass rapidly through my body, trying in vain to ignore their banter.

'I said, "This is out of order,"' the older one of the pair related. '"I'm being victimized."'

'So the screw says, "Well, how many tests have you had so far for suspicion?"

'"Five," I tell him.

'"An' how many were positive?" he says.'

By this time he could barely contain his laughter.

'So I tell 'im, "Er, five."'

And then the two of them creased up.

I squeezed hard. Suddenly the door to the sample-room opened. Before the officer could beckon in anyone else, I volunteered, 'I'm ready!' and jumped to my feet.

Inside (behind the stall, plastic beaker in position, watched by the convex eye), it was soon obvious that I wasn't ready at all. But after five minutes with the officer holding down one of the washbasin faucet buttons I managed to produce the necessary. 'About time,' said the officer, taking the sample from me with a surgical-gloved hand and holding it up to the light. 'That's it,' he added. 'You can return to your wing now.'

The consequences of a positive test can be acutely debilitating: a month on 'basic' (twenty-two-hour bang-up, no association); closed visits (which means that visits are shorter and less frequent and have to take place in a special section of the visits hall behind sealed glass windows and in full view of those enjoying normal visits); and a possible stopping of pay and visits to the prison shop.

Outside, the two young men were still amusing each other. I cringed. The last thing I needed was a mix-up with the samples. Walking back to the wing, emotionally (and physically) relieved, I heard more laughter coming from the waiting area. It echoed in the corridors behind me and then faded.

Yesterday I received my result. There was no need for me to have been concerned about mix-ups. Mr Turnlock, my case officer, called me to the wing office and presented me with a splendid facsimile of a congratulatory certificate informing me in fine copperplate that my urine sample had tested negative.

25 May 2000

Free for a day

You witness many unforgettable moments during a long prison sentence. Some are good, some are not so good. Here's a good one.

I first saw Nathan Jones in a high-security prison more than thirteen years ago. He was a tall, lean, ruddy-faced man with deep-set eyes and a cleft chin and he had a curious way of holding his arms slightly bent and rigid by his sides with his fists clenched – as if to say to anyone brave enough to engage him in conversation, 'Go on then, disagree with me.'

We had never been friends back then. We were barely on nodding terms. Nathan was the type of prisoner other prisoners did their best to avoid. He was just too angry-looking.

It came as no surprise then when I found out that he had done most of his time the hard way. Virtually the only time he'd spent out of solitary during one seven-year period was when he was in the back of a van full of prison officers, often trussed up in a body belt, on his way from one segregation unit to another.

But time passes and people change and someone somewhere had obviously decided to give Nathan a chance. The year before last he was transferred to this medium-security prison, preempting my own arrival by several months.

It was about a week after I landed that I bumped into him again. I'd gone to the gym for a spell on the exercise bike. After peddling with my head down for about twenty minutes, I looked up and there he was, standing in front of me.

'All right?' he said, his lips parted in a half smile. I was struck by how little his physical appearance had changed. Same ruddy face, same bent arms, same clenched fists.

'Er, yes thanks,' I replied.

'You remember me don't you?'

He was looking me straight in the eye. I wasn't at all sure that it was safe yet to disagree with him, so I hesitated, trying to think of a quick way to extricate myself from his company.

'It's Nathan,' he said. 'Nathan Jones.'

'Oh er, yeah,' I said. 'Nathan. How's it going?'

'It's going great,' he said. 'Just great.'

His Welsh lilt was warm and friendly. He was clearly pleased to have found a familiar face from his earlier years in prison, and I felt small. Over the following weeks, however, Nathan and I met often, usually walking and talking around the exercise yard. I learned that before coming to prison he'd been an oil-rig worker in the Middle East and that he spoke almost fluent Arabic. This was not the man I'd earlier envisaged. So how had he survived all those years in segregation blocks? 'I just switched off,' was all he would say about it.

Recently Nathan was told that he'd been passed for a 'day out', a rehabilitative measure designed to help men who have spent a long time in prison adjust to the outside world again. 'My head's in bits thinking about it,' he said, fists clenched tighter than ever.

Last week the big day arrived. The previous day he'd been called to 'reception' (the entry- and exit-point of all prisons) to be issued with civilian clothes. His own had rotted beyond wear many years earlier.

'Jeans and trainers?' the reception officer had asked him. 'Or jacket and trousers?'

'I came in dressed like a man and I'm going out dressed like a man,' Nathan told the officer firmly but politely. 'I'll have the jacket and trousers please, and the shirt and tie.'

He told me later that he'd hardly slept that night. And who could blame him? This was going to be his first unfettered journey into the outside world in more than eighteen years. The prison officer accompanying him would also be dressed in civilian clothes, and for six hours they'd be wandering the local town together, trying out the normal things that normal people do.

On the day, a staff shortage meant that we were all banged up before Nathan was due back late that afternoon. But there were no newsflashes about escaped convicts on the radio that night so I assumed that all had gone well.

The following day I went out to the exercise yard and Nathan was waiting for me. 'How'd it go then?' I asked, though the smile on his face told me the question was unnecessary. 'It was fine,' he said. 'Just fine.'

I'd never heard such peace in his voice. As we walked he relived his taste of freedom, relishing the experience all over again. He'd walked by the river, had a meal in a restaurant, and spent a good hour browsing around the market. At one point he popped into a newsagent to buy some magazines.

'While I was waiting in the queue to pay,' he said, 'I noticed two women who kept looking across at me. I was getting paranoid, until I heard the one say to the other, "I'm telling you, he's a copper!"'

Nathan roared with laughter as he told me this. And then I realized that his arms were relaxed, and his fists were unclenched.

8 June 2000

The oldest con on the block

There are two prime requirements for coping with a prison sentence: youth and good health. Hoagy Smith enjoys neither. We haven't seen much of Hoagy around the jail of late. Mostly he just stays in his cell, reading paperback Westerns or doing crosswords from giant puzzle-books. He's not so mobile now. He can barely walk thirty feet without getting out of breath. And no wonder: he has heart disease, liver trouble, arthritis and skin cancer.

The only way he gets off his wing these days is if he can persuade one of the younger prisoners on his spur to push him in his wheelchair – which is why it doesn't happen very often.

Last week I bumped into Hoagy in reception. I was there to be issued with a new identity card, and he was sitting in his wheelchair by the processing counter, waiting to be taken to the outside hospital. As I approached he turned and nodded. There seemed to be a lot less of him than the last time I'd seen him.

'How's things, Hoagy?' I said, trying to sound cheerful. The maroon tracksuit he was wearing looked ludicrous with his old head poking out of the top. His round face appeared greyer than usual and the licks of silver down on his bald head were uncharacteristically dishevelled. Worst of all, the malignant melanoma on his scalp was weeping a brown residue which glistened under the fluorescent lights.

He shook his head slowly before answering in a whisper, 'Not too good… I've got fluid on me lungs now.'

While I searched for an appropriate response, the two escorting prison officers arrived, jangling keys. Firmly, but with an underlying tone of gentleness, the officer in charge of the escort said, 'You'll be on the closet, Smith.' He placed a small blue holdall upon the counter and said, almost apologetically, 'It's the rules, I'm afraid.'

As Hoagy and I looked on, the officer pulled a five-foot length of heavy-duty chain and two pairs of handcuffs from the bag. Making a noise like a string of exploding firecrackers, the several kilos of shiny metal snaked out of the bag and crashed on to the counter.

When the bag was finally empty an awkward silence descended upon us all. The closet chain is normally used to allow able-bodied prisoners and the guards to whom they are cuffed a measure of dignity during toilet excursions. On this occasion, it appeared to be having the opposite effect.

Hoagy turned to the lead officer, and smiling cheekily said, 'All that for me?'

With the tension broken we were all able to smile as the officer proceeded to fasten one of the heavy bracelets to Hoagy's wrist.

'Just in case you decide to make a run for it, you'll have to take him with you,' the officer said, as he attached the handcuff on the other end of the chain to his colleague.

The jokes helped to ease a difficult situation for everyone, but the irony was lost on no one: the wheelchair designed to mobilize the disabled – the handcuffs and chain designed to hobble.

Once satisfied that he was secure and the paperwork was in order, the reception officer gave the go-ahead for Hoagy's departure. I walked alongside him as far as the heavy steel gate leading to the 'sterile area' (forbidden ground to unescorted prisoners), where the van with blacked-out windows was waiting.

'Take it easy, Hoagy,' I said. The officer on wheelchair duty rubbed the old man's shoulder as he manoeuvred him through the gap.

'Never mind "take it easy",' Hoagy replied. 'It's me birthday in a couple of days.'

'Oh yeah?' I said. 'Which one?'

'See if you can guess by the time I get back,' he said, and winked.

A few days later I was talking to Felix the Gambler, and Hoagy came up in the conversation. Felix told me that Hoagy had served twenty-one years of a life sentence and had then been released 'on licence'. 'But it's a liberty what's happened to him now,' he said.

After seven years of freedom, Felix explained – during which time Hoagy had managed to get himself a small bungalow and a car – his parole officer had decided to revoke his licence and have him recalled to prison.

Nobody knows the reason for the recall, but whatever it was Hoagy doesn't believe he should have been returned to such a secure environment. So far he's been back inside for just over a year.

'Do you know how old he is?' I asked Felix. When he told me I was stunned.

I'm curious now to know how it all went wrong for Hoagy. But when he gets back I won't mention it. I'll just guess his age at sixty-five, and look surprised when he tells me he's eighty-three. I wonder if he knows that he's the oldest man in the prison? I won't mention that either.

22 June 2000

A football hogfest in the TV room

In prison, football is king. Second only to rumour and specula-tion about fellow prisoners, it is the most talked about topic in the exercise yard. During the season the weekend revolves around it. Throughout the week workshop tea breaks are spent dissecting the previous weekend's action and slagging off the latest winners of the numerous premiership sweepstakes. (An 'item' is used as a stake – either a £2 phonecard or a chocolate bar, depending on your social circle.)

So it was with a level of excitement only marginally less than that generated by the prospect of the World Cup that Euro 2000 was anticipated. For three weeks there would be a veritable hogfest of almost twice-daily football, ensuring that all unhappy thoughts about being in prison would be firmly relegated to the back of the mind.

There was some consternation on our wing, however. The governor made it clear that the football would not be allowed to dominate the television room. 'We're not having the minority suffering for the sake of the majority,' he announced one Sunday lunchtime. It meant that if anyone voted for the other side during one of the late-evening matches then, no matter how few their number, over it would go.

Since there are only two television rooms, it was hoped that the television normally dedicated to showing films taped from the satellite movie channels might be made available for the late-evening matches. But this was without acknowledging the sentiments of George the video orderly (also known as 'Pig-headed George'). George, unfortunately, hates football.

'He thinks he owns that fucking video,' is a common criticism whenever he refuses to tape a specially requested film or programme (usually on the grounds of 'that's crap').

But the criticism is never to his face. For everybody knows the story of how George 'weighed in' three gangster types in a maximum-security Midlands prison in the eighties. Though it was a long time ago, the fact that George had been stabbed six times by the three before he mounted his retributive ambush (a week later, with a steel bed-leg) made his reputation safe for ever.

As far as George was concerned Euro 2000 was also 'crap' and as there was nobody on the wing strong enough to challenge him it looked like much of the live action might have to be listened to on the radio.

That was until the apparent formation of an unlikely (and some would say unholy) alliance between Big Rinty and Felix the Gambler. Nobody will forget the atmosphere in the TV room when the big Dundonian turned up to watch the first Scotland v England match. His face plastered in a woad-like substance divided by a white saltire, he looked like an incarnation of William Wallace himself. All that was missing was the claymore and the sporran. But instead of crying 'Freedom!' at the final whistle, Rinty screamed 'Bo-lucks!' and stormed out of the room.

Everybody expected Rinty to take a back seat after Scotland were knocked out. Instead he hung around and slagged off the England team at every opportunity. 'But we'd have supported Scotland if they had gone through instead of England,' said several of the England fans. '*Bo-lucks!*' re-emphasized Rinty. And, whenever Rinty was ranting about the 'English poofs', Felix the Gambler always seemed to be in the background – offering odds of 10-1 against England making it to the final. Phonecards changed hands like nobody's business.

And so with feelings stoked high by the dodgy duo's dubious shenanigans a unanimous TV-room vote for every match was virtually guaranteed. Hmm...

Hooliganism was the big issue when England played Romania. Three murderers in the back row complained that it shouldn't be allowed. 'Those yobbos are giving us a bad name over there,' said one, as others in the room nodded in agreement. Then, when Phil Neville gave away the penalty, all eyes turned accusingly towards Luby (Luby Lou, the Jew), the only Man United fan in the room. Luby just sat quietly, clutching his bird-cage on his knee (inside which Schindler, Luby's budgie, also kept a heedful silence).

But when Ganea scored and sealed England's fate the room erupted. Luby and Schindler almost disappeared under a hail of used teabags and crushed soft-drink cans.

The real drama, however, unfolded on the night of the final. The room was quiet and well behaved until half-time. With Italy one goal up against Germany Felix offered 3-1 against victory for the brave Umbrians. The temperature rose as phonecards and IOUs were thrust feverishly into the notorious risk-taker's open palms. When the officials showed four minutes of extra time, the cry went up, 'Felix, Felix, Felix'. That was until Wiltord scored the equalizer. Then, when Trezeguet scored the golden goal, a sense of disbelief seemed to pervade the air like the smell of silage from the local farms.

Felix stayed cool. He just stood up and announced with a cackle, 'They thought it was all over – it is now.' And then he turned and walked out of the room, laughing.

6 July 2000

Hoagy gets released

Ragby is the governor's tea boy. ('Boy' is stretching it a bit, mind you, as Raggers is in his forties with a long, grey ponytail and a complexion like rendered concrete.) He's good at 'overhearing' while distributing tea and coffee among the VIPs and so also enjoys the exalted role of unofficial camp herald.

One day last week I was walking in the exercise yard wondering when the sun was going to shine, when there was a tugging at my shoulder. It was Ragby.

'Have you heard?' he said excitedly.

'No,' I said, 'what's happened?'

'Hoagy Smith has been released on compassionate grounds.'

Before I could question him further, Raggers was halfway across the yard relaying the information to other parties.

I thought a lot about Hoagy after Ragby told me the news. That night I did some calculations and worked out that he must have been sentenced in 1971. He would have been fifty-four at the time, a relatively late age to receive a life sentence.

The next day I spoke to a few of the other old-timers and tried to get a flavour of what life must have been like for Hoagy in those days. By all accounts it was different to life inside today.

Without exception everyone wore prison uniform: blue-and-white-striped cotton shirt, denim jacket and trousers. (Definitely no white leather trainers or designer tops – and almost no illegal drugs.) Short back and sides was the regulation haircut and discipline was enforced rigorously by blunt-talking prison officers, the majority of whom were ex-military personnel. In some prisons even talking in the exercise yard was forbidden.

Conditions varied. Some jails allowed prisoners an hour or so out of their cells in the evening for 'association' on the landing: TV, darts, cards. In others the best you could hope for was your statutory hour of outside exercise, as long as the weather was not 'inclement'. There were no telephones on the landings, and no toilets in the cells – just a bucket, emptied in a communal sluice each morning at the call for 'slop-out'. (I recall that experience myself, but only for my first eight years inside.)

The main sources of employment were the 'mailbag shop' (sitting in rows, hand-sewing mailbags, eight stitches to the inch, no more, no less); and the 'grommet shop' (sitting in rows, hand-fashioning hemp fibre into plumbing washers). Hoagy would have known all about mailbags and grommets. In 1982 he would have been sixty-five and – just like on the outside – eligible to retire. Perhaps he worked on, as a cleaner or a 'tea boy'. Whatever he did, it kept him active for the next ten years until his release in 1992, aged seventy-five. It must have been a shock when he was recalled.

The other day a few of us were talking about Hoagy and somebody mentioned the morning a little while ago when he'd been summoned over the Tannoy for a visit from the probation officer who had had him recalled to prison. Apparently the officer wanted to check on the old man's 'progress'. A prison officer had pushed Hoagy over to the visits hall in his wheelchair and left him by a table in the middle of the busy hall.

When the probation officer, a young woman, entered and sat down opposite him, Hoagy gripped the wheels of his wheelchair. Heads turned and the hall went quiet as, with what must have taken an almost superhuman effort, Hoagy began to inch the chair around, slowly, slowly, until his back was facing the young woman.

'He should have got a round of applause for that,' somebody

35

said, and we all nodded. We were gathered by the wing bulletin board underneath a 'notice to prisoners' from the governor. The notice informed us that Hoagy had died in hospital the night before – three days after his 'release on compassionate grounds'.

There's a rumour going around that the authorities knew Hoagy only had days to live and that his discharge was really on the grounds of financial and administrative expediency. But who cares? At least he was free when he died.

20 July 2000

In prison you make friends at your peril

You meet a lot of people inside, many of whom become acquaintances, associates or even, occasionally, allies. But contrary to what some on the outside believe, it's rare that you make friends.

I remember early on in my sentence, thirteen or fourteen years ago, having a conversation with the man who lived in the cell next door to mine. I listened as he recounted the argument he had had with his girlfriend during a visit that day. Before storming out of the visiting room with the argument unresolved, his girlfriend had yelled, 'It's all right for you; you're in here with all your friends.'

'Can you believe that?' he said, as we leaned against the safety rail outside our cell doors, looking down on a group of fellow prisoners engaged in a game of pool. 'Friends?'

I was relatively new to prison then. My neighbour was more experienced. I thought him cynical, bitter perhaps. In time, however, I have come to understand what he meant. That is not to say that nobody ever makes friends in prison. But true friendship is a precious relationship, not to be entered into lightly. In prison you do so at your peril.

Take what happened to a young prisoner in here recently. Joey Bowker's troubles began last summer. While on remand, and later while awaiting allocation following his conviction for conspiracy to supply drugs, Joey had made 'big plans'.

He was ten months into his six-year sentence when he arrived in this jail. His high expectations were quickly frustrated, however, when he discovered the dearth of work opportunities. A scarcity of outside contracts meant that several of the big workshops were having to operate with a scaled-down workforce. Not that Joey especially wanted to work. He just needed access to customers. If he wasn't working he was locked in his cell – which meant limited contact with other prisoners. The bang-up was costing him 'serious money'.

Then, one night last November, Joey met Japes the Joyrider in the payphone queue. 'Can't get a job?' asked Japes. 'If you don't mind sitting behind a sewing machine for nine quid a week I'll have a word with our gaffer.' Joey was grateful. Bright prospects beckoned. 'Thanks,' he told Japes. 'You seem like good stuff. Maybe we could do business together?'

During the following weeks and months, from behind their sewing machines, Joey and Japes shifted the three grams of 'brown' (heroin) smuggled in during each fortnightly visit by Joey's wife, Sue. For a while business was good.

Then came disaster. Sue was caught on the visiting-room CCTV cameras as she spat the clingfilm-wrapped drug into a crisp bag ready for the handover.

As prison officers from security sprinted through the crowded room, scattering children's toys and coffee trays in their wake, Joey made a lunge for the crisp bag. He was hoping to swallow the evidence but panicked and fumbled. Seconds later the prison officers were on him.

Detained by the triumphant prison officers in a classic 'control and restraint' lock – bent at the waist, arms behind the back, wrists secured and head held steady – Joey could only watch from the corner of one eye as Sue was led away sobbing. 'I love you, babes,' he managed to call, but she never looked back.

By the time Joey emerged from the segregation block, Sue was in Her Majesty's Prison Holloway and the two children were in a foster home. For the twelve weeks that Sue was in custody, Joey leant heavily on Japes for support. He shared Sue's letters with Japes and allowed him to admire photographs of Sue in which she had revealed herself for her husband's eyes only. 'These are a bit near the mark,' Joey explained, 'but you can look, you're a friend.'

When Sue was released she was reluctant to visit Joey. She still wrote to him and spoke about the future but she was taking no chances. She was just grateful to be out of jail and back with her children.

In the meantime, Joey's drugs operation had collapsed. Then Japes had an idea. 'I'm due some ROTL,' he said (release on temporary licence). 'I'll go and see Sue and bring us back a parcel' (a clingfilm-wrapped drugs stash, concealed inside the rectum).

Japes took his 'temporary' leave last month. Few were surprised when he failed to return. But it was tough on Joey, especially when he received Sue's scribbled note. 'Dear Joseph, me and the kids are moving up north with Denzil. Don't try to find us. We are starting a new life.'

A week ago Joey Bowker took a drugs overdose. We watched from the exercise yard as they wheeled him out into the ambulance on a stretcher trolley. Thankfully it turned out to be more of a cry for help than a genuine suicide attempt. And now he's back, recovering in the prison health centre. In a couple of days they'll return him to his cell on the wing. But there's still no word from Joey's friend, Denzil Japes.

3 August 2000

All the time it takes to map out revenge

Even though it took place nearly two years ago, I still remember the meeting. It was so unusual. I was standing halfway along the teatime meal queue when I felt a firm tap on my back.

I turned around and found a dapper, moonfaced Asian man

with bright eyes and a long black beard. I'd been in this jail for only a few days, but I recognized the man as someone who lived on the same spur, a few cells along from mine.

'How do you do?' he said, offering me a hand. 'My name is Hosni; in here they call me H.' Instinctively I shook his hand, but immediately I regretted it. For all I knew, I was shaking hands in public with the most unpopular man in the prison. During the coming months I learned that, although he was not especially unpopular, people were wary of H. He was 'always praying' they'd say, or he was 'always talking about conspiracies'.

One day he approached me on the landing. Shifting his eyes as if he was about to offer me a bargain from the back of a lorry, he reached into the pocket of his denim jacket and produced a cassette tape. 'Here,' he said. 'Listen to this.'

Not wanting to appear impolite, I took the tape and thanked him. It turned out to be a recording of a lecture by someone with an American accent. Something about AIDS being an experiment by the West which had got out of control in Africa. Three days later, I went to his cell to return the tape. It was lunchtime and his cell door was ajar. I could hear voices inside so I knocked and pushed the door open.

The window was covered with a blanket and the light was off but through the gloom I could see H sitting on the bed. Another Asian man I did not know was sitting on the only chair. On the table I noticed a neatly folded ornate prayer mat, along with a heavy-looking tome I assumed to be the Koran, and a small white cap. The two men stopped talking and looked at me.

'H,' I said. 'Your tape.' He took the tape from my outstretched hand, then spoke to his associate in his own language. Turning back to me, he said, 'I was just telling him about the day you introduced yourself to me in the servery queue.' Thinking he was kidding, I smiled. But he remained stern-faced and held my gaze, and I knew he was playing a little mind-game. From then on, I too was wary of H.

A while later, I heard that he and another fellow had been sacked from their jobs as visits-hall cleaners, following the disappearance of a box of chocolate bars. Each blamed the other for the theft and a silent feud developed. H got a new job outside, keeping the prison grounds clean. But his former workmate remained unemployed and on 'bang-up' (twenty-two hours a day in his cell) until his transfer a few weeks later.

The feud should have ended then, but an associate of the man who had been shipped out, a man called Jenkins, decided to prolong it on his associate's behalf. Jenkins and a couple of henchmen would block H's path on the stairs, push in front of him in meal queues, or utter racist comments whenever he passed by.

About a month ago, the attrition came to a head. H returned from work one day to find slices of that morning's breakfast bacon on his bed and, worse, on his prayer mat. Jenkins was the prime suspect. The confrontation between the two was eagerly anticipated. Surely it would be the mother of all tear-ups? But H did nothing. Not even an angry glower. Maybe he was biding his time, everyone thought.

It seemed he'd missed his chance when, two weeks later, Jenkins was frogmarched off the wing by the burglars. Under his bed they'd found a bedsheet that had been torn into strips and plaited, along with a detailed plan of the perimeter fence. The tip-off had been slipped anonymously into the wing postbox.

Jenkins protested vehemently that the stuff had been planted, but his denials did not stop his immediate ship-out 'in patches' (blue-and-yellow escapee garb). On the landings, however, people are not quite convinced. 'Jenkins only had six months left; why should he want to escape?' they ask. 'Only someone who worked in the grounds could have drawn such an accurate plan,' they point out.

The most compelling testimony comes from the man who worked in the laundry-exchange store. Last Saturday morning H could not explain why he had only the one bedsheet to exchange. 'It's lost,' was all he was prepared to say.

It seemed a bit too obvious to me. But then again, perhaps that was his intention.

17 August 2000

Game show's hard cell

It was Slippery Al who first voiced what many were probably thinking as we sat in silence in the darkened television room watching the third or fourth taped episode of *Big Brother*. Sitting bolt upright and pointing at the screen, he exclaimed, 'It's just like they're in prison!'

He had a point. A group of strangers confined in a relatively cramped living space, their every move observed and commented upon; bickering among the inmates; a little paranoia; secret snitching sessions behind closed doors; and even psychologists employed to offer 'scientific' interpretations of behaviour. (And yes, just like in prison, these interpretations and opinions are often contradictory.)

But as far as a true comparison between the *Big Brother* show and prison is concerned, the similarities are superficial. The difference is fundamental. For a start the *Big Brother* contestants have committed no crime. Not even 'nasty' Nick Bateman – of whom one of my neighbours, eleven years into a mandatory life sentence, said last week following the former public schoolboy's eviction, 'That Nick's a dodgy bastard.'

There are more differences: the contestants are volunteers, vying with each other to win a prize of £70,000; the group is of mixed sex; they can fraternize intimately, drink alcohol and prepare their own meals with food of their own preference. Sure, they have to abide by a set of rules and are subject to an external controlling influence. But they can also reach democratic decisions on internal issues during group meetings around the dining table. If all that wasn't enough, they even get freshly laid eggs each day (or they did do before the hens contracted diarrhoea) and they can sleep outside under the stars whenever they wish. The biggest difference of all, of course, is that at any time they choose the *Big Brother* contestants can simply pack their bags and leave. What luxury.

'Imagine,' said Slippery Al when I spoke to him over a cup of tea in his cell a couple of days ago, 'if they had something like a *Big Brother* competition set in a prison, with a prize for whoever manages to escape.'

Yes, I thought, imagine that. And now it seems we might not have to imagine it for much longer. Apparently, plans for just such a show are at an advanced stage. At this very moment, in a secret location 'somewhere in England', a mock prison is being constructed for the show, and contestants are being recruited. Already I have an image in my mind of Big Rinty getting yet another knock-back from the parole board after twenty-one years inside, dancing out of the governor's office waving his hands Al Jolson-style and singing, 'It's only a game show, it's only a game show...'

No doubt there are sections of society that will welcome such 'entertainment'. And who can blame the producers? Real life docu-soap television has proved to be a mainstay of prime-time programme scheduling in recent years. It appears that modern television audiences just cannot get enough of watching themselves in everyday situations. *Big Brother* was the next step. But I can think of many reasons why *Big Brother* in prison is a step too far. Firstly, never before has the issue of crime and punishment been so much at the fore of public and political debate. Prison is at the heart of the debate and should not be allowed to be undermined by the whimsical notion that it can in some way be equated with knockabout game-show fun.

We're living at a time when suicides and incidences of self-harm in prison are at an all-time record level. Last year there was, on average, one self-inflicted death every four days in a British prison. Only a couple of weeks ago a prison governor resigned his post at a young offenders' institution because of 'Dickensian conditions' that he could no longer tolerate. Now I'm not advocating sympathy for those in prison. For every prisoner rightly convicted there is at least one victim. But it's inconceivable that anyone who has suffered at the hands of another would be comfortable with such trivialization of their tormentor's punishment.

The Bishop of Liverpool, James Jones, described the *Big*

Brother show as 'a human zoo'. Given the present state of the prison system, how much more abhorrent would he find a similar show set within the confines of a fake prison? Prison has the potential to be a genuine community resource. Until society achieves that goal it should have no truck with anything that treats the issue of imprisonment as just another titbit of game-show trivia.

24 August 2000

A quiet Sunday morning, three years ago today

I woke up late that day. My getting-up routine on a Sunday morning usually began when the alarm on my watch sounded at 7am. Normally I would reach out blindly to where the watch lay on the chair by the side of the narrow bed and press the alarm's stop button. I'd then switch on my radio, which I would also have placed on the chair the night before, and lie listening to the news while waiting for the cell door to be unlocked at around 8am. As soon as I heard the sound of boots approaching and keys jangling I'd jump out of bed and pull on shorts and flip-flops. By the time the key was turning in the lock I'd be standing with towel and soap in hand, ready to exit the cell and hurry to the shower room.

The reason for the rush was because I knew that in a cell across the landing from mine Deaf Dave would be going through a similar procedure. There were no cubicles in the shower room, just a row of bare showerheads jutting out of the tiles. The feeling of being exposed and vulnerable was least apparent under the shower in the far corner nearest the back wall. Whoever was first in invariably bagged that one. On Sundays it was always a race between me and Dave.

But that morning I slept in. It had been a bad night. In the early hours a man in the segregation unit had become hysterical and had started screaming like a maniac out of his cell window. The seg unit was about forty yards away from the high-security long-term wing where I was located. The man's howls echoed around the deserted, spotlit prison grounds, bouncing off the twenty-foot walls and shredding through the wire-mesh fence that encircles the exercise yard (situated directly outside my window). I had woken with a start. Others, mostly younger men on the short-term wing, who had also been woken up by the racket, began shouting out of their cell windows, cursing the disturbed man.

'Shut the fuck up, you fraggle.'

'Quiet, you nutter.'

My neighbour at the time was a man who had been in prison since 1975. He had escaped several years earlier and spent two years on the run before being recaptured. Following his taste of freedom, he found it difficult to come to terms with long-term imprisonment. 'I proved I could live a trouble-free life out there,' he used to say, during his more lucid moments, to anyone who would listen. But his argument carried little weight with the authorities. Perhaps that was why he had developed such a severe persecution complex. Whenever the manic screaming occurred – night-time included – my neighbour, imagining the cacophony was somehow directed at him, would roar back his own tirade, often threatening the anonymous, disembodied voices with torture and death.

Such episodes were not unusual. When they occurred I'd switch on my radio and listen to the World Service. But not that night. Instead I just lay there listening to the voices in the dark, sometimes smiling, sometimes frowning, until the din diminished and sleep returned.

Suddenly, bright rays of sunlight were streaming through the bars of my cell window. I opened my eyes and saw instantly that my cell door was ajar. I was momentarily confused, and then I heard the sound of other cell doors being opened systematically: we were being unlocked for breakfast. Sunday morning, 31 August 1997.

I knew that Deaf Dave would already be under the safe shower and that rushing was pointless. But force of habit made me pull on shorts and flip-flops anyway, grab soap and towel and hurry out of the cell and down the landing. Inside the shower room I could make out Dave's skinny, bearded form in the far corner. 'Mornin',' I shouted, before stripping and diving under a hot jet. Dave's head was covered in soapy foam. That and the fact that his deaf ear was pointed in my direction meant that at first he didn't even notice I was in there with him. I began to soap, and then Dave's voice boomed, 'Have you heard the news?'

'No,' I said. 'I've only just got up. I slept in.'

'It's Princess Di,' he said. 'She's dead.' It sounded like there was genuine anguish in his voice, but I still thought he was kidding. I swore at him.

'I'm telling you the truth,' he said. 'She was in a crash.'

Back in my cell I switched on the radio and Dave's news was confirmed. It was unbelievable. All day the atmosphere on the wing was subdued. It was like Christmas Day, only worse. It was the same the day after, and the day after that. The effect of the princess's death lasted for weeks. For so many years she had brought glamour to drab prison wings via television news reports and tabloid newspapers. By rejecting the rules of the establishment the princess too appeared to consider herself something of an outlaw. Her maverick behaviour and non-judgemental attitude added to her attractiveness for many in jail.

The princess left me with a miserable legacy however. Every anniversary of her tragic demise, it seems I'm destined to be reminded of my morning shower with Deaf Dave.

31 August 2000

Squash and cake with Eugene

It was Eugene's sixty-ninth birthday the other week. You would never have guessed it by looking at him. I knew he had some sort of problem with one of his hips and that that was why he always took his stick with him whenever he went to the exercise yard. But the smooth olive skin on his face and his thick, dark hair gave the appearance of a man ten or even fifteen years younger.

I didn't know Eugene very well. He hadn't been on the wing for very long and lived on the spur above mine. Apart from a polite nod to one another in passing, the only conversation we'd had before his birthday had been in the day room a couple of weekends earlier. He'd been sitting at a table by the window putting the finishing touches to a miniature chapel he'd built from matchsticks. He noticed me watching him and beckoned me over.

'You've got patience,' I said, smiling.

'It helps me pass the time,' he replied. The model was a beautiful piece of work. It must have taken him months. 'Here,' he said, lifting off the roof. 'What do you think?'

The floor was polished wood. Red and green velvet carpeting separated the rows of painstakingly crafted pews. There was an altar, a font, and even a couple of lecterns complete with tiny Bibles. Most impressive of all was the hand-painted triptych behind the altar.

'You must be a very religious man,' I said.

He frowned, and then smiled as he replaced the roof and said, 'I don't know if I am.'

We didn't get the chance to speak again until the evening of his birthday. It was a Monday. I was walking past his cell and the door was wide open. I glanced inside and saw there were people gathered. Eugene was sitting on a stool near the back wall. He saw me and called out, 'Come in, come in.'

Inside, I recognized Wicks, Eugene's neighbour and workmate, sitting on the bed. I knew they shared a bench in the 'domestic appliances for the blind' workshop, assembling talking microwaves and talking clocks. Next to Wicks sat Slippery Al. Two others from Eugene's spur were standing chatting.

I sat down on the bed and Eugene passed me a cup and began

filling it with orange squash. On his table there were plastic plates laden with slices of swiss roll, biscuits and peanuts. Pointing at the food he said, 'Please, help yourself.'

It was Wicks who explained that it was Eugene's birthday. 'Wow,' I said. 'Many happy returns, Eugene.' And everyone lifted their cups and drank.

I sat facing the picture board on Eugene's cell wall and couldn't help but notice all the photographs displayed of children at various ages: in living rooms; in gardens; at parties. He saw me looking and said, 'My religion – grandchildren,' and we laughed at our private joke.

I don't recall speaking to Eugene again that week. The following Saturday I woke up early. I'd been dreaming that I was standing by a black cab with its engine running. When I opened my eyes I could still hear an engine ticking over. I reached up and looked out of my cell window. There was an ambulance parked on the grass with its back doors wide open, but no sign of a patient. I got back into bed and wondered what had happened.

Later, in the breakfast queue, I learned that the ambulance had been for Eugene. He'd been taken to the outside hospital. A heart attack was suspected. When I spoke to Wicks he told me that it wasn't Eugene's first heart scare. He also told me that they had known one another a long time. 'We started off together in the Scrubs nine years ago,' he said. 'He's a gentleman – my best mate.'

The next day we were all called to the day room and Mrs C, our landing officer for that day, informed us that Eugene was dead. 'He had a massive heart attack this morning,' she said. We shuffled together uneasily and Wicks cried.

When a fellow prisoner dies naturally, the mood becomes philosophical. The consensus is that it's unwise to dwell too much on a loss; much better to focus on the positive side.

'He's gone to a better place.'

'He's free.'

'He won't need that stick any more!'

Wicks organized a collection amongst prisoners and staff, which raised £160 for the British Heart Foundation. Slippery Al got everyone to sign a condolences card for the family.

Unexpectedly, last week the prison governor invited Eugene's two daughters into the jail. He even showed them around personally. There were tears when they were shown their father's cell, and again as they stood by his workbench. But Wicks was allowed to meet them and they seemed reassured that their father had had such a good friend inside.

This was a sincere conciliatory gesture by the governor, and many were lifted by it. For my part, I keep wondering about Eugene's matchstick chapel. I hardly knew him, and I know it's none of my business, but is it too much to imagine that it might be in the care of one of his grandchildren?

14 September 2000

All that graft for nothing

Nobody was really surprised when, at the beginning of this year, Johnny Beggs was transferred across to the enhanced wing. Most agreed that he'd made a spiffing effort to reform. Anger management, alcohol awareness, drug education – he'd attended all the offending-behaviour courses (and he had the certificates displayed on his cell wall to prove it). 'I'd do the advanced fackin' knittin' course if it would convince these people that I'd changed,' he said before he secured his cushy move.

Evidently 'these people' had been convinced, for the cell doors are never locked on the enhanced wing. Neither are there bars on the windows. Beggsy was confidently anticipating a move to 'open conditions' in the near future. Parole was on the horizon. That was, until Ray Kyte arrived.

'Ray's a good friend,' Beggsy announced reassuringly when he introduced Kyte to several associates one day in the exercise yard in early spring. 'We go back years – he's staunch.'

But this was a different story to the one he'd told Felix the Gambler a week or so before Kyte was due to arrive. During a 'meet' in the library Beggsy confided that someone he knew had been allocated a move here and it was causing him some concern. Without mentioning a name, Beggsy told Felix that the man was 'a right dodgy geezer' and that there were a few good people 'doing big bird' (long sentences) because of him.

The problem was that the two men had been friends in the past. They had been brought up on the same 'manor' (neighbourhood) and at some stage in their careers had been involved in several of the same 'bits of work' (robberies).

Beggsy's dilemma was a difficult one. 'He doesn't know that I know he's been working for Old Bill,' he explained to Felix, 'so he's bound to expect us to pal up together when he gets here. But how can I have it with a wrong 'un?'

Felix's advice was to be cautious. 'You're well established on the enhanced wing now,' he said, 'away from all the bollocks of the main wings. Give your acquaintance a polite acknowledgement, but keep your distance. Before you know it you'll be in an open jail and you can put this lot behind you.'

Beggsy appeared grateful for Felix's wise counsel. 'That's it,' he said. 'That's what I'll do.' But Felix was not convinced. Something about Beggsy's manner told him that whoever the new arrival was Beggsy was fearful of him, and not just because he was 'dodgy'.

So he was not surprised when Beggsy sidled up to him in the gym several days later and said that he'd made a mistake. 'That bloke I told you about,' he mumbled. 'I got it wrong. It's his cousin who's the wrong 'un.'

'I just gave him the glazed look,' Felix said to me as we walked and talked about it in the exercise yard the other day.

With his athletic form draped in designer sportswear, gold chains and hundred-pound-plus trainers, Kyte presented an impressive image. He was the kind of prisoner other prisoners either loathed or admired. But during that initial introduction he held no sway with Felix. Now I knew why.

Felix more than anyone must have wondered what Beggsy was up to when he began to further Kyte's cause with prison staff. His alleged reformation had given him a measure of credibility in the eyes of the authorities. He was trusted. He was believed. 'We were at school together,' he told the manager of the enhanced wing. 'Trust me, Ray Kyte will be an asset to this wing,' he argued on numerous occasions.

It took a few weeks and a lot of eyebrows were raised. But sure enough – despite having attended no offending-behaviour courses, nor having shown any other evidence of a desire to reform – Kyte suddenly appeared in the enhanced wing.

It should have been a good move for a man with three or four years still left to do. But Kyte had other ideas. Pine beds and a television clearly meant little to a man of his calibre. Loyalty to a friend, if that's what Beggsy was, meant even less.

A couple of weeks ago, using outside help, Kyte escaped – 2am, rope ladder, vehicle waiting. The aftermath was inevitable. Within days Beggsy was summarily turfed off the enhanced wing. To add to his ignominy, a couple of days later he was shipped out to a local jail known as 'the dustbin'. No open prison. No parole.

'I wonder if he took his offending-behaviour certificates with him,' Felix said to me as we continued walking.

'I doubt it,' I said. In my mind I had an image of the man now occupying Beggsy's cell on the enhanced wing. I could see him ripping the certificates off the wall and hurling them into the bin.

All that graft for nothing.

28 September 2000

Reason and rehabilitation

On the move to a new prison

'Pack your kit,' said Mr Turnlock, who was in charge of the wing office when I returned from morning labour one day last week. 'Your movement order has come through.'

I knew a transfer was on the cards. It was a hole I had dug for myself eighteen months earlier, soon after my arrival in this jail. During an introductory interview with an acting deputy governor, the issue of offending-behaviour courses had arisen.

'The only course I truly felt challenged by,' I told him, 'was enhanced thinking skills.'

'Really?' noted the deputy governor, a kindly mannered and obviously educated man.

It was the truth. I had genuinely enjoyed the ETS course. But when it had first been suggested to me in the previous establishment I'd been in, I had been sceptical. Surviving fifteen years on the wings and landings of high-security prisons with mind and body intact seemed to me to be evidence in itself that my thinking skills were hardly in need of enhancement.

'Who's going to run that, then?' I had asked the wing probation officer who'd called me to his office to discuss it. 'Richard Branson?' Much to my subsequent mortification, the probation officer had replied, 'Er, no. I am, actually.'

In fact, the course turned out to be a blessing in disguise. Mundane repetition is the staple diet of prison life and I hadn't realized how much I had been affected by the torpor it engendered – nor how complacent I had become.

The programme took place in the prison psychology department. Every morning for six weeks I was one of a group of ten cons being tutored in the philosophy of Edward de Bono and the like. Conflict resolution by negotiation; cooperation and mutual advancement; logical problem-solving; consensus through discussion; cost–benefit analysis.

Apparently, people in industry pay 'thousands' to attend similar courses on the outside. That was all well and good, but I didn't truly believe I now needed a further such course. It was just that the move to this place had been such a big step towards freedom that I was eager to assure those in charge that accepting me into their wonderful prison had been an excellent decision. (I'm blushing at the memory.)

'I only wish,' I said to the deputy governor before I could stop myself, 'I only wish that there was another perhaps even more challenging course available so that I could build on the skills I learned on the ETS.'

After a moment's thought, and much to my chagrin, he replied, 'Actually, there is such a course – "reason and rehabilitation" – but it would mean a temporary transfer to another prison at some stage in the future as we don't run it here.'

My heart sank. 'Oh great,' I said, forcing what I hoped looked like an enthusiastic smile. 'Put me down for that then.' I knew I had overplayed my hand, but it was too late to backtrack. Why couldn't I have kept my big mouth shut?

And now the time had come. I spent the next few days getting my gear together. Not that I had that much to pack. Since the introduction of 'volumetric control' in the mid-nineties, a prisoner has been allowed 'in possession' only what will fit into two regulation property boxes (about 2ft x 2ft x 8in). Any surplus must be handed – or sent – out of the jail, or else it gets shipped to Branston in Staffordshire, where the prison service has a depot dedicated to the storage of prisoners' belongings.

Before volumetric control, long-term prisoners were notorious for carting numerous transit boxes packed with years of accumulated paraphernalia from prison to prison. Some even saw it as a mark of status. In those days you could tell a lot about a new man arriving on the wing just from the amount of kit he was lugging. Twenty-two boxes? You knew he had been around, you could guess his history; respect.

On the morning of my departure Big Rinty and the Guru helped me to carry my stuff to reception. The reason and rehabilitation course was set to run for twelve weeks. There would be a settling-in period of about a month at the new jail, and then a post-course debriefing a month or so after it finished. I was looking at six months away, I guessed.

'It'll pass,' said the Guru as the reception officer directed me into one of the holding rooms. 'Drop us a line,' said Rinty. 'Let us know the score.'

These days nearly all prison transfers are undertaken for the prison service by outside contractors. I shook hands with my two pals and then sat down and waited for Group 4 to arrive.

12 October 2000

Surprises behind the blue door

Prison-to-prison transfers always generate mixed feelings in the person being transferred. It's good to have a break in the routine and get a glimpse of the outside world (even if it is through the tinted window of a Group 4 sweatbox cubicle). The respite is only temporary, however. You may have left the frying pan, but you know as sure as hell that all that beckons is a fire.

As the van skitted through the Midlands countryside I tried not to think too much about the prison I was headed for. Instead I stared out of the tiny window and concentrated on the fields and the trees and the traffic.

We had been travelling for a little over two hours when the van turned off the main highway and into what looked like an industrial estate. After a few left and right turns we dipped into a tree-lined avenue, at the end of which I could see a high, steel-clad fence topped with razor wire. Suddenly I felt the caterpillars crawling in my stomach, waiting to turn into butterflies.

Fifteen minutes later I was standing in front of a white-topped counter in the small, brightly lit reception area, with my cardboard box and two polythene bags of belongings at my feet.

Two prison officers on the other side of the counter checked my transfer paperwork and then signed for my acceptance from the two Group 4 guards. Turning to face me and nodding towards my stuff, one of the prison officers asked, 'Anything in there you shouldn't have?'

'No,' I said, as the Group 4 guards walked past me on the way back to their van.

'Load it on to that, then,' he said, pointing to an upright trolley leaning up against a radiator, 'and follow me.' I managed to balance the box and the bags on the trolley and off we trundled down a corridor with green-painted walls and black gloss skirting. We reached a steel gate and the officer unlocked it and swung it open for me. I pushed the trolley through the gap and found myself in the middle of an even longer corridor with the same colour scheme.

'Straight down there,' said the officer pointing left. 'You'll see a blue door at the top of three steps with "B Wing" above it. Give it a kick. They're expecting you.'

It was midday and I assumed that most of the jail was banged up. So far I hadn't seen another prisoner. I knocked on the blue door as instructed. There was a rattle of keys on the other side and it was unlocked and opened.

'You the lodger?' said a young fresh-faced prison officer.

'Er, yes guv,' I said.

I pushed the trolley on to the wing and immediately sensed the heavy, fetid atmosphere. 'You'll be all right on this wing,' said the officer, grinning. 'It's for long-term men only.'

I gave him a mouth-only grin and said nothing. I knew of course that even if this young man were to spend the next thirty years on the landings in his uniform he would still be no nearer a real understanding of 'long-term men'.

I parked my gear by the wing office and then an odd thing happened. I heard someone coming down the central staircase and when I looked up I recognized him immediately. 'Grady!' I exclaimed. So this was where his clash with Bruce the Aussie earlier in the year had brought him. How strange, I thought, that he should be the first prisoner that I encounter here.

'How's things?' I said as he approached.

'Excellent,' he replied. 'This place is a lot better than that other shit-hole,' he continued. 'What are you doing here?'

'I've just come to do a course,' I said. 'Reason and rehabilitation. I'll be here for around six months.'

'I've done that course,' he said. 'It's good. I came out top of the group.'

Christ, I thought. Although I didn't think I really needed the course, I had come determined to give it my best shot. But if what Grady was telling me was the truth, his 'success' did not bode well for it at all. He asked if anything had been said after his departure from the other place. I hadn't the heart to tell him how much rejoicing there had been at his downfall.

'Nobody said a word,' I fibbed. He seemed pleased about that and then explained that he was a wing cleaner, and that that was why he was unlocked.

As he walked away I noticed a tall black guy with short dreadlocks emerge from what I later learned was the laundry room where he was the washing orderly. He looked about thirty and had a serious bodybuilder's physique. He caught my eye and started walking towards me. I thought he was going to try to tell me that he was 'the main man' around here, or something like that.

My heart rate accelerated. Since I was going to be here for a while I would have to stand my ground, let him know I wasn't weak. Adrenaline pumping, I got ready for a 'don't fuck with me' stare-down. But, instead of being hostile, when he reached me he bent forward and picked up my two large bags of kit. 'You're on my spur on the twos,' he said. 'Twos' meant the second floor. 'Let me give you a hand.'

Wouldn't you just know it? You prepare yourself for a fight, then within seconds you're saturated with relief and it takes all your self-control not to burst into tears. With my defences melted and my spirits lifted I followed the big man up the stairs. His gesture was the best welcome I could have hoped for.

19 October 2000

Bumping into trouble

The man who helped me carry my bags to my cell told me his name was JJ. 'You know Toby Turner?' he said, as we shook hands by the cell doorway.

'Yes I do,' I replied.

'He's up on the threes,' he said. 'He heard you was comin' here and asked me to look out for you.' Moments later the landing officer arrived and banged me up.

I wasn't sure that Toby being here was good news. It had been more than four years since I'd seen him. Aged seventeen, he had been sentenced to be detained 'during Her Majesty's Pleasure' (HMP is the junior equivalent of a life sentence). When he was twenty-one he was 'starred up' and transferred from a young offenders' institution to the adult maximum-security dispersal system. Soon afterwards he became attached to an IRA crew, running errands and looking after the hooch.

Toby had been brought up in care homes and the IRA men were like the uncles he never had. But it wasn't just a surrogate family thing: something had happened in those care homes. As a result Toby hated all forms of authority with an unbridled ferocity. Being seen to 'side' with the 'Irish cause' was his way of demonstrating his utter contempt and loathing for 'the system'.

Those of us who knew him well, though, knew that the hard-core persona was just a front. He certainly hated authority figures – the fifteen counts of assault against prison officers which he had acquired over the years were testament to that. But beneath the aggressive body language and big talk he was a vulnerable, emotionally stunted adolescent. The fact that he was now in a medium-security prison meant that he was at least making some progress. Hopefully he had matured during the years that had passed since we last saw each other.

When the cell door was opened at teatime for the evening meal and 'association', Toby was waiting for me out on the spur. 'Now then!' he said, grinning from ear to ear.

His appearance had not changed a bit. Same shaved head, same dark-tinted aviator-style glasses. He wore shorts and flip-flops, and an old grey T-shirt covered in tiny burn holes. I sensed he wanted to hug me, so I got the handshake in first – gripping tight, forcing the space to remain between us.

'How are you, Toby?' I said.

'I'm all right,' he said. 'It's the others.'

He invited me to eat in his cell. We collected our food from the servery and Toby made a big deal of acknowledging the other prisoners as he showed his 'old friend from dispersal' (the high-security system) the ropes. On the way up the stairs to Toby's cell we passed Grady going down.

'All right?' Grady asked me.

'Yeah, thanks,' I said.

Toby turned his head sharply to face me and said, 'You don't know him do you?'

'Kind of,' I replied.

'What a nob 'ead,' he said. 'He's never out of the fuckin' office.'

Inside Toby's cell a small Indian guy was sitting cross-legged on the bed, watching a portable television perched on a table under the window.

'Sal,' said Toby, 'this is a mate of mine from dispersal.'

'Hi Sal,' I said, and shook his proferred hand. I sat next to him and joined him in watching the evening news while eating.

Toby remained standing. 'Sal always comes up to watch the news,' he explained. 'I'm not "enhanced" (highest privilege level), but they gave me a telly to keep me quiet.'

It was clear that Toby was not making as much progress as I'd hoped. He went on about the prison officers being on his case all the time and giving him grief – the same old chestnuts.

'But you've got to meet them halfway,' I said. 'At least go through the motions, for Christ's sake. You're thirty-one years old. If you don't make the effort nobody will want to help you.'

'I've tried,' he said, though I knew that he knew that he hadn't tried hard enough.

I decided I would try to spend some time talking to him while I was here. It might help, it might not. But one of the worst things in prison is to see young men wasting more years of precious life than is necessary.

'Anyway,' said Toby, 'do you want to see my new party trick?' I looked at him suspiciously. I expected something weird but I was not at all prepared for what happened next. Without warning, he pulled down the front of his shorts, flicked his lighter, and suddenly his pubic hair was a mass of rapidly spreading flames. 'For foork's sayke!' exclaimed Sal, revealing a heavy Scouse accent. 'I'm tryin' to watch the foorkin' news 'ere.' Toby just howled with laughter, while I winced as he beat the flames out with his bare hands.

26 October 2000

The trouble with Toby

Serving a prison sentence is not something that comes naturally. How to survive once you find yourself 'inside' is something you have to learn to do as you go along. It's a good idea to not get involved too much in all that is going on around you. This, however, is easier said than done.

One morning soon after my arrival for the first time ever on a long-term wing, I met a man in the breakfast queue who insisted on relating a conversation he had had with the wing governor on the day that he had 'landed' earlier that week. The man was known to the governor from previous sentences.

'Take my advice,' the governor had told my new acquaintance. 'This time don't get involved.'

'But governor,' the man had replied, 'that's like lifting the lid off a pan of vegetable stew and saying to a piece of carrot, "Carrot, don't get involved with the rest of this stew."'

It was a good point, well made, and the message has remained with me ever since. Only the other day, when Toby Turner presented me with his latest party trick, I had cause to think about it yet again.

The last time I'd seen Toby, more than four years ago, he was still boasting of the '200 blades' (hatchets, swords, knives, axes, machetes etc.) which the police had found in his flat when he was first arrested; and he took special pride in informing people that 'not one was a virgin'. During the short time that I've been here, I've been having most of my meals in Toby's cell, along with Sal, Toby's friend. While Sal watches the evening news on Toby's television, Toby and I talk. I gently try to offer ways ahead with the authorities. Perhaps the anger-management course, I suggest.

'I've done it six times,' says Toby.

'Well, are you using what they teach you?' I ask.

'Course I am,' he answers indignantly.

'No you foorkin' don't,' interjects Sal, without taking his eyes off the television. 'What about last week with Mo on the servery and the chips?'

'That was different,' says Toby. 'He was stitchin' me up.'

'No,' says Sal, looking up from the television and pointing at Toby, 'let's have it right. You was putting pressure on 'im to give you extra and he said, "You can take as many as you want, but I can only give you the one scoop."'

'And what did you do then?' I asked Toby.

Sal interjects again. 'He told Mo that he would see him in the recess later and stick his scoop up his foorkin' ringpiece.'

To his credit, Toby looks embarrassed, but it's obvious that he has still got a lot of work to do before he can make further progress through the system.

A couple of mornings ago I was mulling it over again and wondering about the wisdom of 'getting involved' in this situation. In prison a man must serve his own time, in his own way, I reminded myself. Maybe it was time to start easing myself away from Toby's company.

Breakfast time was nearly over. I was drinking a cup of tea and listening to the news on the radio when there was a knock on my cell door and Toby pushed it open.

'I need to talk,' he said. 'I've just been in the governor's office. The police are coming to see me.'

'Sit down,' I said, and he sat down on the end of my bed.

'It's about what happened to me when I was a kid in the home,' he said. 'One of the other lads who's my age has made allegations about some of the care staff and the police want to interview us to see if it happened to anybody else.'

Toby sat with his head bowed as he told me this. He started to tell me more, and then his upper body began to shudder and I realized he was crying. I understood immediately that those tears had been a long time coming. I placed my hand lightly on his shoulder, and I cried too.

9 November 2000

Toby lays his ghosts to rest

There has been a dramatic change in Toby's demeanour since that first visit from the police. It has only been a short time: just over a week. But already there is consistency in Toby's behaviour. No more off-the-wall joke-telling or unexpected party tricks. No more rants at prison staff or slamming of cell doors.

The police have instructed him to concentrate on remembering as much as possible about his time in the home. He has been given exercise books in which to jot his recollections. 'We know it's difficult, and may be painful,' the smartly dressed young lady police officer told Toby, 'but we need names: who did what to whom? And how often? Be as specific as you can.'

It seems like a tall order to me. A lot to ask someone in Toby's situation: thirty-one years old, fourteen years in prison, not much light at the end of the tunnel. Perhaps they know how hard he has become. But do they know how dangerous life in prison can be once you lay down your armour?

Toby's 'normal' prison behaviour can be unnerving sometimes. His unpredictability can turn the mood of a whole wing. I watched a documentary once about a community of monkeys who lived in a jungle clearing. Just like in jail there was a natural hierarchy among the males: two or three who were dominant, a few relatively passive middle-rankers, and the remainder adolescents and infants. Occasionally there was rough play and sometimes more serious jostling for position. But, in the main, all the monkeys understood and respected the order of the community and conducted themselves accordingly.

That was until one of the adolescents found a biscuit tin which had been discarded by the filmmakers. Instinctively he picked up the tin and started to bang it. The rest of the monkeys were so startled that they fled in all directions. In that instant, the power of the hierarchy had been usurped.

Toby's unpredictability always had the same effect in the prison setting. It was a most effective survival tool.

Sometime soon, Toby is to be taken to a purpose-built unit in a police station, where specially trained officers, backed up by counsellors, will take his statement. He has to be discreet. If it gets out on the landing that Toby is 'cooperating with the police', all kinds of rumours and speculation will erupt. Only me and Sal – who has been in and out on several sentences since he and Toby first became friends in a punishment-block exercise yard over ten years ago – know what's going on.

At teatime unlock we meet in Toby's cell to eat our evening meal. The three of us sit on the edge of Toby's bed. Me and Sal watch the evening news on Toby's portable television, while Toby pores over his exercise books – scribbling here, crossing out there. I'm just wondering how he is going to cope with prison life once his ghosts have been laid to rest.

Having said that, there was an indication of things to come after an incident a couple of evenings ago. We were sitting in our usual positions in Toby's cell when suddenly the door flew open and in burst Grady.

'I've been attacked!' he yelped, before pushing the door to and plonking himself down on the toilet-pan cover. In an instant Sal was off the bed and inserting a wedge under the cell door. Toby covered the spyhole and I turned the sound down on the television. For a long couple of minutes only Grady's heavy breathing was audible. Then Sal's voice exploded in his direction. 'You foorkin' arsehole! What do you think you're doin' bringing trouble to this door?'

'Leave it Sal,' said Toby, grabbing his friend's raised arm. 'Give him some space.'

As Grady talked, it emerged that he had snitched on Mo, the 'number one' on the servery, for stashing surplus cartons of breakfast milk instead of giving it out as seconds. Mo had confronted Grady in his cell and roughed him up, but in the fracas Mo had sustained a bruised eye and so looked as if he had come off the worst. As Grady fled, Mo had threatened to 'chib' him (a chib is a home-made stabbing instrument).

Suddenly Toby took command. 'Come on,' he said calmly to Grady. 'I'll walk you to your cell and then I'll go and see Mo.' Sal looked at me as Toby loosened the wedge. I shrugged.

I don't know what passed between Toby and Mo that evening, but I do know that Mo would never have stood for a threat. The next morning I was behind Grady in the breakfast queue. Mo was serving the Cornflakes, black eye and all. When he saw Grady he nodded. 'Mornin',' he said as he filled Grady's bowl. 'Forget the milk business,' he added. 'It's over.'

A learned man once wrote, 'Two men looked through prison bars, one saw mud, the other, stars.' I'm convinced. Toby Turner is beginning to look upwards.

23 November 2000

Prison works in mysterious ways

Talk about short notice. I was cleaning out my cell on the twos landing when I heard my name being called from the ones. It was mid-morning and everyone was either at the workshops, on education classes, or behind their doors. Only the wing cleaners – one of whom I had recently become – were unlocked. I squeezed out the mop and gave the cell floor a final wipe. A minute or so later I was standing in the open doorway of the wing office.

Inside were three prison officers. Mr Phelps, bald and broad-shouldered, was standing reading a newspaper; Mr Duffus, slim and bearded, was checking prisoners' meal-choice slips; and senior officer Mr Dodds, a corpulent pipe-smoker, was sitting at his desk writing in the large red daybook. I tapped gently on the door frame and said to nobody in particular, 'Did someone call for me guv?'

Only Mr Dodds acknowledged my presence. 'Ah, yes,' he said, laying down his pen and picking up a memo sheet. 'We've had this through from the movements clerk; Group 4 will be picking you up in half an hour.'

The fact that I was returning to my allocation prison came as no surprise. I had gathered as much during an uneasy meeting with the wing manager a week earlier. But to spring it on me just like that meant that I would not be able to say any goodbyes.

'But…' I began, before second thoughts cut in. Experience had taught me the pointlessness of trying to rationalize the irrational. Resigned to the suddenness of the move, I lifted up my chin and went back upstairs.

As I gathered my things together I reflected on the situation. OK, I had been sceptical about the reason and rehabilitation course, but a healthy scepticism is essential if you are to remain sane during a long prison sentence. Even though I didn't think I needed it, I hadn't been totally disingenuous when I'd volunteered for the course. It would allow me to demonstrate a commitment to using my time constructively whenever the opportunity arose, I'd reasoned with myself at that moment – and, perhaps more importantly, it would provide several months of quality interaction and mental stimulation.

I did explain this fully when I was interviewed for an hour and a half by two of the prison-officer course tutors who visited me several months before my transfer.

'And you enjoyed the enhanced thinking skills course?' asked the young female officer.

'Yes I did,' I said emphatically.

'A lot of what we do is similar,' she said, 'but our course is slightly longer and, we feel, more challenging.'

I had to fill in numerous forms and questionnaires during the interview. These would be assessed.

'There are only ten course places available,' the same officer explained. 'The assessment will tell us if you meet the criteria.'

This eased my conscience. The final decision would be based on objective professional judgment.

I half expected to get a knock-back when the notification came later in the year. But no – the assessment apparently indicated that I warranted a place. So what had gone wrong?

Two weeks ago I had a cordial meeting with the same female officer who had been present during the initial assessment interview. She presented me with a 'compact' (no drugs, no disruptive behaviour, respect for other course members and tutors), which I happily signed. Only for the wing manager to call me to his office a week later and drop his bombshell.

'I'm sorry,' he said, 'but we've made a mistake. You shouldn't be here.'

'But...' I began.

'You've already done the enhanced thinking skills course,' he continued. 'If we had known that, you would not have been offered a place.'

'But...' I began again, and then I hesitated. But what? I couldn't tell him anything about the assessments and interviews I'd had that he didn't already know. It was all logged in their paperwork. My mind was a blur. Was he serious? Or was this a cunning plan devised by prison-service boffins to test my reaction?

'I've been on to movements,' he said, 'and we're going to get you back as soon as we can.' He was serious.

In the van on the way back I thought about my pals Toby and

Sal and all that we had shared over the past few weeks. It pained me to imagine them returning from morning labour to find me gone – cleared out without a word.

On my return to this place there was cause for good cheer however. I was located back on the same wing and, thanks to Mr Turnlock, in the same cell. On the night of my return I treated Big Rinty, Felix the Gambler and the Guru to a large jug of coffee while I recounted my adventure.

We talked until bang-up and then, as they were leaving my cell, I said rhetorically, 'What is this all about?'

'Ah,' responded Felix, stopping in the doorway, 'that's the wrong question. But I'll tell you the right answer, if you want it.'

'Go on then,' I said, remembering his interest in Buddhism and other esoteric schools of thought.

He looked at the three of us and, smiling, said, 'Endure.' We smiled back. As usual Felix had told us what we already knew.

7 December 2000

I spy a warder being extra watchful

'Merry Christmas,' said Mr Turnlock, as he lifted the flap covering the observation panel on my cell door at around 7.30 on Christmas morning. He was not being facetious, though there are some that can be. More than once I had been on a wing where it was considered a jolly jape to turn up the volume on the Tannoy system before the cell doors are opened on Christmas morning and yell, *'Happy Christmas campers. Ho! Ho! Ho,'* and other such fun spoutings. Effective wake-up calls for sure, but not especially welcome to most 'campers' on that particular morning of the year.

This year, though, our landing patrol officer was a man confident and humane enough to extend a little warmth. As Mr Turnlock checked the rest of the cells for the morning count and roll check, everybody who was awake got a cheery 'Merry

Christmas'. His sincerity made for a good start to the day.

Breakfast was good: beans, scrambled eggs and bacon. But thanks to Binch, a bespectacled antipodean doing four years, queuing for it was an ordeal. Wearing a green-and-yellow paper hat, Binch insisted on wandering up and down the queue bellowing 'Wasssuuup?' and blowing a party screecher into people's faces. Big Rinty was not amused. 'If he comes near me with that thing,' he said, scowling, 'I'm gonnie ram it doon his throat.'

Sitting around our dining table, Felix the Gambler was in a lighter mood. As we tucked in, he told me and Rinty that during the night he'd had a dream about a Boxing Day race meeting. In his sleep he'd seen a gelding called Boss Man win. 'I'm telling you,' he said, 'this is it.' Apparently the horse really existed and was due to run the next day. Felix had some knowledge of its form. 'It lost last time out,' he explained. 'But that was after winning a race twenty-four hours earlier. This time it's been rested properly. In my dream it romped it by two lengths.'

An hour or so later Rinty and I went out for a walk, leaving Felix salivating over his form-book and a borrowed tabloid race-meeting pullout. His 'arrangements' would be conducted by phone via trusted and loyal friends.

It was cold but bright outside. Except for a couple of damson-coloured clouds drifting lazily, the sky was clear. There were no more than a dozen men in the exercise yard – most would be sitting in warm cells playing cards or board games, or huddled in television rooms watching *The Shawshank Redemption* on the video channel as it was piped through from the central control room.

The fact that the yard was almost deserted was no bad thing. The constant competition for space can be wearying sometimes. Space is the real luxury in prison. Standing guard in the corner of the yard, dressed from head to toe in black waterproofs, was the unmistakable rotund form of prison officer Mr Watchwell, who normally worked in the punishment block.

'What's he doing?' said Rinty, pointing at the officer, who was stamping his feet.

'He's probably trying to get the circulation going in his legs,' I said.

'Not that,' he said. 'Look – he keeps calling up at that cell window and then looking about him as if he's lost something.'

We walked in Watchwell's direction until we were within earshot. 'Your turn,' said a ruddy, steam-breathing face pressed against the bars of the top floor window. Watchwell looked around at the concrete, the tarmac, the fence, the razor wire and then said, 'I spy with my little eye...'

'For fuck's sake,' spluttered Rinty. 'They're playin' I-spy!'

Back on the wing, Felix was incredulous when we told him. 'You know what?' he said. 'It sounds like that Christmas Day during World War I when the opposing sides ceased hostilities and had a game of football.' Not quite on the same dramatic and poignant scale as that experienced by those valiant men, I know, but there was no denying that he had a smidgen of a point.

At lunchtime Binch was at it again irritating the dining-hall queue with his screecher. Nobody needed reminding that it was Christmas, but I'm almost ashamed to admit to the meal we were served: soup, then turkey and stuffing, with sprouts, carrots, roasties and mash, followed by fruit, a mince pie, and a slab of Christmas cake. The prison kitchen, as usual on such occasions, had done us proud.

There was no bang-up during the day, so most of us retired to the TV room for the afternoon to watch *The Green Mile*. (Films about innocent men wrongly convicted and sent to jail always go down well inside.) After the film there was a brief interlude – long enough to collect a 'cold tea' from the servery – and then it was time for *Titanic* on BBC1. After the blockbuster came bang-up and bed. Another Christmas was over.

And Boss Man? Well we listened to the race on Boxing Day. Apparently he's still running.

28 December 2000

Cody's long wait for freedom

Good news this week. (Good news travels fast in prison, though not as fast as bad news. That's because, for many inside, bad news is often better received than good news, just so long as it is addressed to somebody else.) As usual with the big scoops it was Ragby, the governor's tea boy, who was first to report.

The other day he was in the governor's office serving herbal tea to a group of Ukrainian penologists (over here on a fact-finding mission) when the governor's fax machine started humming. The memo which appeared in the in-tray was marked 'confidential' but it might as well have been marked 'for the attention of Mr Ragby'.

By the time he reached the exercise yard he was breathless. 'It's Cody,' he wheezed at the two off-duty kitchen workers who were walking in front of me and Big Rinty. Ragby rested his hands on his thighs and gulped down a couple of lungfuls of air before adding, 'He's got his Cat D!'

I suppose we should have rejoiced. This was very good news indeed. After twenty-three years of mainstream prison life Cody had finally been given a squeeze. 'Cat D' meant recategorization to 'suitable for open conditions'. In a couple of years he could be walking the streets a free man.

Of course we were pleased for him. Everybody was. But there was a lot of sadness too. For ever since Cody began his life sentence in 1978 he has been protesting his innocence. His last appeal was in the early eighties. It failed because the 'fresh evidence' that he believed would clear him was not presented to the court in time.

He never gave up. Year after year he petitioned the authorities. Then, three years ago, a new independent body charged with investigating alleged miscarriages of justice agreed to look into his case. I wasn't acquainted with Cody then, but by all accounts there was no question of 'cautious optimism'. As far as he was concerned, with an independent investigation under way he was home and dry. All that remained was the calculation of the compensation.

But these things are never quite so straightforward. The independent body began looking into Cody's case in late 1998. After countless communications, notifications and clarifications it looked like a decision was imminent last autumn. But still the weeks passed with no answer.

Everybody who knew Cody was rooting for him. The delay served only to raise hopes even higher. What a Christmas present this was going to be, everybody thought. Yes. What a Christmas present.

I met Cody's family last summer. It was during a special family-visit day and I was helping out at the tea hatch. Cody's son and daughter and his daughter's partner were up. His son and daughter are in their late thirties now and his daughter has daughters of her own. He introduced me when I took them over a tray of tea.

As I shook hands with his loved ones, Cody nodded towards his daughter and said to me, 'You know what?' Cradled in his arms was his three-month-old granddaughter. She was sound asleep and looked as safe as the Bank of England. 'She was just fourteen when I came away.' I took my eyes off the baby and smiled awkwardly. 'And now,' he continued, 'she's got a fourteen-year-old daughter of her own.'

This was obviously the blooming adolescent sitting next to him with her face pressed hard against his shoulder. I smiled awkwardly again. I wanted to say something encouraging, something hopeful. Instead I said it was nice to meet them all, and left.

Back at the tea bar I wanted to kick myself. Why didn't I tell that son and daughter how well their dad was managing this strange life? And how irrepressible he is, and how generous and funny?

Cody received the decision from the independent review body by special letter on 18 December. The investigators, it said, were 'not minded' to refer his case back to the Court of Appeal. That was it. His Christmas present.

But it didn't stop him helping Felix the Gambler and the other kitchen lads prepare the food for the New Year party held in the visits hall each January for the local old folks. Felix and Cody volunteered as servers on the night and me and Big Rinty volunteered too. We had to wear hats labelled 'I'm Rinty' and 'I'm Felix'. Cody wanted to make us all laugh and wrote, 'I'm Cody – and I'm innocent!' We couldn't help but oblige him.

Is Cody innocent? Who knows? But one thing is certain. Now that he's got his Cat D, he's going to get another chance.

11 January 2001

Does prison work?

At the time of this article, January 2001, almost 63,000 people were living behind bars in Britain, equivalent to the population of Guildford.

I can still vividly remember his dark, pinstripe suit, so skilfully tailored that it retained its immaculate shape even when he sat down, and his lightly tanned, manicured hands emerging from stiff white cuffs. It was the summer of 1990 and Lord Justice Woolf, as he was then, had come to visit the high-security Midlands prison where I was being held. The visit was part of his inquiry into the Strangeways riot and other prison disturbances.

At that time the prison was well known in the system for holding mainly 'hardcore' offenders. Long sentences and cramped accommodation made for a tense atmosphere. Wing life could be perilous with a stabbing or a scalding almost every other day. 'Paranoia City', the inmates called it. Lord Woolf had already spoken to the governors and the prison officers, and now he wanted to talk to the prisoners.

There were about thirty of us present that morning, serving sentences ranging from five to thirty-five years. We sat on soft-backed chairs set in three semi-circular rows in the prison chapel. After some polite small talk, Woolf explained why he was there. 'We need to try and find out what it is actually like to be in prison.'

Until that moment, this was not something I had spent much time thinking about. What was it like to be in prison? Didn't he know? Of course he didn't – how could he? For the first time since beginning my sentence six years earlier, I contemplated the fact that the people responsible for sending us to prison had no idea what it was like. Perhaps that was the problem.

Around me, men I had never before heard discussing their feelings about prison were doing their best to fill in the blanks. It was 'educational', one said.

'In what way?' the judge wanted to know.

'Well, you learn to understand yourself better,' came the reply. 'You spend so much time in your head.'

Others talked about the loneliness, the fear, the paranoia. I sat there and drifted back to my first day as a prisoner. I'm walking along a gantry-style landing on the long-term wing of a large London prison. I'm on the third floor: 'the threes'. I'm carrying a plastic bucket inside which clatters a plastic cup, knife, fork and spoon. Under my arm I have a 'bedroll': two flannel sheets rolled up inside two coarse blankets.

I'm guided to my cell by a large prison officer sporting a handlebar moustache. The peak of his cap has been 'slashed' to fit low over the bridge of his nose. We reach the cell and with a noisy rattle of his keys he unlocks the door and pushes it open. He's smiling. 'In you go son, don't be shy.' The door slams shut behind me.

The cell is dimly lit by a small, grime-covered fluorescent light. The walls are covered in cracked and flaking emulsion. There's a table, a chair, and a metal bed with a stained mattress and half a foam pillow. The heavily barred window high up on the wall is closed, and the urine-tainted air makes me want to retch. I sit down on the bed. Time to collect my thoughts – but no, I hear a sound like rolling thunder approaching fast, and suddenly the cell door is unlocked and pushed open again. 'Slop out and get your tea,' instructs the officer.

A stream of denim-clad men in identical blue-and-white-striped shirts are shuffling past my door. I step out and join the flux. Down two flights of metal stairs to the ground floor, we head towards a set of trestle tables. A row of prisoners in white are serving food. Before I get there I am stopped in my tracks by a scream.

'He's fuckin' dead meat!'

'Nonce! He's fuckin' dead meat!'

I turn and see two men: one wields a mop handle, the other a metal bucket. They are using the domestic implements to beat a third prisoner, who cowers in a cell doorway.

'He's fuckin' dead meat!'

Suddenly I'm aware that no one else is stopping. Nobody is intervening. Few even look in the direction of the violence. I fall back in line, pick up a tray, collect my meal and return to my cell. As I sit on the chair and spoon down the food, all thoughts and feelings about why I am in prison are relegated. My first priority, I now understand, is to learn to survive.

Back in the chapel, a prisoner was telling the judge that life inside was 'a war of survival'. I recognized the angry voice instantly: it was John, who lives on my spur. The same John who during a riot a few months earlier had led an attempt to burn alive a number of sex offenders. John's accomplice had been transferred out of the prison following the riot but he had remained, his status with other prisoners enhanced. I half wished that somebody would explain this to the judge, and say, 'Your Honour, that's what prison is like.'

The judge's visit set me thinking. Prison was no doubt necessary. But it was unsettling that prison life was such a mystery to society. There seemed an assumption among many on the outside that people in prison were inherently different. Prisoners were seen not as individuals, but as a collective, with the same crude standards, values and culture – a sub-race, almost.

It made me think about some of the people I had met inside. I remembered Dave, who on the out had been a postman; Howard, who had been a student; and Tam, who had been a council worker. The four of us used to play pool at the weekends. Tam was nicknamed 'the Commander' for his midfield prowess in the wing football team. Dave had asthma so he'd taken up jogging. He'd lost six stone, bolstered his health and begun doing sponsored runs around the football pitch for charity. Howard spent his days in the education department, studying and dreaming of becoming a teacher. Three and a half years later, my next movement order came through. By then Tam had been transferred to Scotland. Dave was in a semi-open prison, let out regularly to take part in charity road-runs. And Howard was dead from a diabetes-induced coma. One night he went to sleep with his face in his pillow and never woke up.

Prison life is mostly a continuous repetition of the same day, over and over again. Finding a purpose and a meaning beyond 'punishment' can be a struggle. Often people are not in prison long enough to discover anything worthwhile beyond a new set of criminal alliances. Or people end up inside for so long that any good that might have been achieved along the way is undermined by bitterness and resentment.

The paradox of imprisonment lies in society's expectations: the community wants retribution, but also rehabilitation. For many, sending people to prison is not enough – they must suffer while there. But only somebody who has never been to prison would believe that jails are 'soft' places.

I remember the campaign a few years ago calling for prisons to be made more 'austere'. But the truth that the austerity brigade failed to grasp is that the harsher a prisoner feels he has been treated, the less of an obligation he will feel to abide by society's rules – and the more likely new victims will be created after his release. Official figures speak for themselves: more than 50 per cent of prisoners reoffend within two years of release. I have seen it with my own eyes: a young man serving four years, and not prepared to kowtow to what he sees as the intransigence of the prison regime. Why can't he go out in the exercise yard when it's raining? Why has his mother not been allowed to visit him just because she brought the wrong visiting order by mistake? He gets known as a 'troublemaker', goes 'on report', and loses his 'time off for good behaviour'. Less than two years after he is freed, he is back, serving a minimum twenty-five-year sentence. Any connection?

A fair answer to Lord Woolf's question would not be entirely bleak. Opportunities for personal advancement abound in prison. I have never been in a jail which did not have an education department, library, gymnasium, chapel, psychologists, probation officers and counsellors. I have been a beneficiary of all the above. When I sat on that bed in that London prison seventeen years ago, I never dreamed how my life would be transformed. I could barely string two sentences together. Now I sit here with an embarrassment of qualifications, which include Braille transcription, sports leadership, a clutch of O levels and an arts degree.

There are many fine people who work in prisons. I recall the cookery teacher who made sure everyone in her class got to make a Christmas cake to send home to their families, even when they couldn't afford the ingredients. The teacher who taught his play-reading group to love Shakespeare. The young prison officer who treated prisoners with such respect that, when he died suddenly, dozens of inmates in their best striped shirts lined the route from the gate to the prison to bow their heads to his hearse. And the governor who had the courage to tell a man convicted of brutal crimes that, in his view, considering the man's background, he was as much a victim as his victims. But the fact remains that I've never been in a jail where making prisoners feel good about themselves was a priority.

Many prisoners were sceptical about private prisons at first. The morality of making profit from imprisonment seemed questionable at best. But the message began to spread that they were preferable to state-run prisons. A conversation with a prison auxiliary helped me understand why. He had transferred prisoners to a private prison. 'You should see the difference,' he said. 'As soon as the cons get out of the van, they're greeted with a "Good morning, Mr Smith, would you like to come this way?" They're reminded that they're people first and prisoners second. Their whole demeanour changes. In return, they're polite to the staff, and to each other!' I had to admit I had never been to a prison like that.

Prison is designed to disempower. Everyone in jail is vulnerable to a greater or lesser extent. Prisoners live at the mercy of those who are in charge, and of each other, and dignity is a scarce commodity. If the regime is characterized by an attitude that undermines a prisoner's confidence and self-esteem, then all the stated good intentions will be worth nothing. It is when prisoners feel that they are not being afforded respect as people that the cynical prison culture – the culture of John and the nonce-beaters – thrives.

During the course of his inquiry, Lord Woolf visited forty-three prisons. When his 600-page report was published there was a surge of optimism through the system. That was until it was all but mothballed by the 'Prison works!' philosophy of the mid-nineties. More people in prison, the theory went, meant fewer criminals on the streets, so fewer crimes being committed.

Before this idea took off, the chaplain in a jail I was in told me, 'Mark my words, in the future imprisonment will be about warehousing.' I witnessed first hand what he meant. Within two years that jail doubled its population, but had its education budget slashed. Staff and prisoner morale collapsed. Similar changes occurred all over the country. Since then prison numbers have soared, as have prison suicides, and the best those who serve society can come up with is more of the same.

Prison can work, but not if the system is overloaded and under-resourced. If it is to work in society's best interest, it is imperative that only those that really need to be locked up, are, and that all prisons work towards a positive regime where respect and dignity for prisoners is not compromised for misguided reasons.

Concerned about the alarming rise in prison numbers, Lord Woolf urged politicians to stop 'playing the jail card'. Those who continue to play it are running a dangerous game of bluff, and there can be no winners in the long run – only more victims.

29 January 2001

Scars that never heal and men you hope never to meet again

'Any movement yet guv?' I was standing in the open doorway of the wing office. Mr Turnlock was on the phone. Twenty minutes earlier there had been a 'general alarm'. I thought I knew the reason why. The orderly who delivers the newspapers from the library had told me. Mr Turnlock finished talking and replaced the handset.

'What is it?' he said.

'Er, any movement yet?' I repeated. 'The stabbing…'

'What stabbing?' he said.

'The paper orderly said there had been a stabbing on one of the wings and that was why movement had been stopped.'

'Rubbish,' said Mr Turnlock. 'You see how rumours erupt in these places? Movement was stopped because an old chap collapsed outside the chapel. It started back up again ten minutes ago.'

'Oh,' I said, 'right.'

Feeling foolish, I left the wing and made my way towards the exercise yard. Mr Turnlock was right. After all these years I should have known better than to believe the worst without question. But the atmosphere in the jail had been a little on the heavy side recently. A week earlier a man had been attacked by another wielding a lino–cutting blade fixed into a piece of dowling. The home–made weapon had been thrust into the victim's face with such force that the steel edge had ploughed deep furrows across the bones of his cheek and jaw. The resulting forty stitches made it look as if he had been flung face first through a car windscreen. I spoke to the victim briefly in the healthcare centre a few days later when I was up making an appointment to see the dentist. It was the worst chibbing I had ever seen.

I didn't know the scarred man, but coincidentally I had spoken to him once before. It was a couple of days after his arrival last September and we were browsing the same bookshelf in the library. He asked me what the prison was like. 'Relatively quiet,' I told him. Unimpressed, he began dropping names of reputed tough-guy prisoners he had allegedly already done time with – 'faces' in the system. The conversation was beginning to bore me until I heard him mention the name Braggs.

'Who?' I said, startled. 'Donny Braggs?'

'No,' he replied, 'his son, Joe. Donny Braggs is dead.'

'You're kidding me,' I said. I pressed him for details. It was important to be sure we were talking about the same man. Satisfied we were, I asked him what had happened.

'He was stabbed in the leg in a nightclub,' he explained. 'Gangrene set in and it killed him.'

'Christ,' I said, and drew a deep breath.

Thirteen years had passed but I had never forgotten my run-in with Donny Braggs. We were on the same wing at the time. Donny was 'on the book' (a Category A prisoner) and was known for his short temper. One sleepy-eyed Monday morning I bumped into him with my breakfast tray outside my cell door. Immediately he began ranting and hurling abuse. His racket was drawing dozens of pairs of eyes in our direction so I implored him to come into my cell. 'The screws will be on us in a minute,' I said. 'Come on, I'll make us a cup of tea.'

He followed me in, but straight away recommenced his tirade. He was becoming hysterical. Realizing I had made a mistake, I grabbed the front of his shirt, intending to shove him back outside. Instead Donny wrong-footed me and swung me around full circle. He reached up behind his head with his right hand and suddenly I felt a stabbing blow in the corner of my left eye. He must have seen my cutlery in a cup on the shelf behind me before pulling me around. Luckily for me the knife he grabbed was only made of plastic.

More blows to my scalp and face followed before instinct caused me to drop my head and unwittingly crash it against the bridge of his nose. Bleeding heavily, Donny then fled from the cell.

We never resolved that conflict. He was shipped out a couple of days later for threatening a prison officer and I explained my swollen eye and the weals on my face by fibbing that I had 'collided with someone while jogging'.

Over the years I occasionally thought about Donny. The prison system is a small world and I couldn't help wondering if and when there would be another confrontation. God knows if he ever thought about me. Although I'm ashamed to admit it, I felt relieved when I learned of his demise.

Thinking about it now, perhaps it was not so foolish after all to have believed the worst from the library orderly. One thing I'm sure of though: for a long time to come, whenever the young man with the forty stitches hears that 'movement has been stopped' he'll be minded to believe the worst without question. And it will be the most natural thing in the world.

15 February 2001

The worst crime? Grassing on fellow cons

One of the first lessons you learn in jail is 'no grassing'. Anybody telling on his fellow cons, or even suspected of colluding with the prison authorities, is treated like a pariah. 'A grass is worse than the worst nonce,' Jack, an experienced prisoner, told me early on in my sentence.

It is a powerful message to those new to prison life; an unwritten golden rule paraded as an aspirational and binding community value. For the uninitiated it gives the impression that access to an exclusive club is on offer – a club whose members adhere to a certain code and behave with a particular kind of honour.

But it doesn't take long before you find out that in truth it's a pretty rotten club. When I parted company from Jack and was transferred north, the prison officer to whom I was handcuffed in the back of the van took great delight in divulging that in that prison Jack was the security department's most reliable source of information.

Of course I was sceptical. Jack had been a respected figure in the jail. As a bank robber he automatically occupied a lofty position in the hierarchy. And he was 'staunch' – always first to bang on his cell door when unlock was late, or to rear up at the servery officers when the food was cold.

There were only two reasons, it appeared to me, why the prison officer should have told me that about Jack. Either it was true and he was trying to educate me in the duplicitous nature of prison life. Or it was false and he was trying to undermine any ideas I might have been forming regarding camaraderie among prisoners. 'Divide and rule,' Jack used to say. 'That's how they keep control.' Was that what the officer was attempting, I wondered. But then I remembered how Jack often spent time in the wing office. 'Family problems,' he would explain. He seemed to have a lot of those.

But what could Jack's motivation be? What about the 'code'? Jack always gave the impression that he was a 'con's con' – a stalwart defender of the prison culture. Doubtless his reports would reflect this. Men like Jack rarely give any serious thoughts to 'rehabilitation'. Did he gamble that, by betraying the secrets of the wing, prison officials would overlook the image and reward him in some way? It seemed a perilous strategy. Life on the landings could be dangerous indeed for an informer exposed.

Eight or nine years later I discovered the existence of the official 'inmate informants system'. The jail I was in had a flourishing magazine. One day someone submitted an article that criticized the informants system and the policy of offering inducements to vulnerable and desperate men. The governor saw it and had the editor effectively arrested and held for seven hours in the punishment block. The amount of detail in the article led the governor to believe that a prison service security manual was loose on the landings. Apologies were proffered, however, when it was found that the revelations had come from a new book on prison law available to all in the prison library.

Later I went to check out the book with the magazine editor. It made spectacular reading. Staff were instructed that prisoner informants should be offered rewards such as incentive bonuses in their pay; the promise of positive recommendations to the parole board; transfers to preferred prisons; or even recategorization, perhaps to open conditions, where town visits and home leaves were possible. The part that really caught my eye was the paragraph explaining that the best informants were 'prisoners who have the respect of other prisoners and who are regarded as above suspicion'. 'It's like a rats' charter,' said the magazine editor. Jack sprang to mind.

I never saw Jack again. But on two occasions I bumped into his best friend, John Feckles. Both times Feckles was serving a different sentence. Like Jack, he purported to be staunch – a noisy finger-pointer always quick to decry and denounce others. Yet despite his obnoxious attitude and no evidence of a desire to reform he always managed to finish off substantial chunks of his time in open prisons. Last week I heard that Feckles was on his way here. When I overheard him being described as 'good stuff' I was tempted to issue a warning. 'I smell a rat', discreetly whispered, would perhaps have been appropriate in the circumstances.

But no. Those who transgress and confide their transgressions in others have only themselves to blame for the consequences. And anyway, I might be wrong about Feckles.

1 March 2001

A friendship comes under strain

'All I'm saying is…'

I was in Big Rinty's cell, sitting on the end of his bed. Rinty was perched on the edge of his soft-backed chair, in the corner, opposite the head of his bed. 'You're saying nothin', 'cos ah don't want te know,' he interjected, poking his half-rolled cigarette at me for emphasis.

I decided to try one last time. 'But Feckles…'

'Fuck Feckles!' Rinty exclaimed. '"He's a nonce. He's a grass." You're as bad as him. I'm telling you – I'm not interested.'

His outburst silenced me. I knew he was under stress because of his psychology call-ups. But I still felt hurt by this accusation. It was undeserved and he knew it. He sat back in his chair and finished rolling his cigarette.

'Fair enough,' I said. He flipped his lighter and lit the roll-up. Soon he was engulfed in clouds of blue smoke.

We didn't speak over the next few days. Since Rinty and I live just a few cells apart, it made life a little more uncomfortable than usual. He was out of order saying what he said, but I refused to blank him. Nothing raises the tension more on a spur than a couple of long-termers falling out, actively ignoring each other and allowing the imagined wounds to fester. Whenever we passed on the spur or met in the meal queue or recess I would nod politely and force a half smile. But I was loath to attempt a conversation. Another angry retort from my pal would only have increased the distance between us. Neither did Rinty blank me. He always acknowledged my nods with the same, and a slight raise of the eyebrows.

All I had been trying to do was to share a little information I'd picked up about John Feckles. He was nobody especially important, certainly not to me. My only knowledge of him came from having encountered him twice before in different prisons. From what I had seen I knew Feckles was into prison politics, and that he was adept at agitating the easily led into food strikes or sit-downs. My view, for what it was worth, was that being around someone like that was likely to make doing time even more unpleasant. That, and the fact that he had been close to Jack who had been in all likelihood a secret informer years earlier, made me feel that his company was to be avoided when possible.

Not that I have anything against informants. Good intelligence is essential to the safety of those who live and work in prison. But prisoners who inform on others rarely do so in order to benefit the community. On the contrary, with such tempting rewards on offer, informants enter a moral fog where falsehood and fabrication thrive and where principles are often sacrificed at the altar of self-interest.

Feckles had only been here a couple of days and already he had a small gang of acolytes. When I first mentioned his presence – only to Rinty, and Felix the Gambler – all I said was, 'A wise man would keep that man at arm's length.' It was all they needed to know.

Within a week of his arrival I learned from a good source that in his last jail Feckles had had his locker broken into. 'Deps' (court depositions) in which it was stated that he had been an official police informant up until 1998 had been stolen and circulated. This was salient information. It was what I was trying to relate to the big Dundonian when he almost bit my head off.

Even though I'd taken slight umbrage at Rinty's attitude I understood that he wasn't really angry at me. He was angry because for the past few months he has been duelling with the prison psychologist – whom he calls 'the astrologist'.

'According to her, I've done nothing positive in twenty-two years of jail,' he said to Felix and me after his last interview. 'All she wants to know is which boxes have I ticked on the forms she keeps giving me to fill in. It's a joke.'

Only it's not a joke. Risk assessment does seem to depend more and more these days on box-ticking and mathematical formulas. Personally, I don't think you can beat keeping a watchful eye and your ears to the ground. Subjective maybe, but I was right about Feckles.

15 March 2001

When Felix chose philosophy

Felix the Gambler lives in the cell next door to mine. As a kitchen worker responsible for preparing the veg diets (his gypsy pie has been known on occasion to lift the morale of the whole prison), he regularly has to start work at 6am. But he is a good neighbour. We have lived in adjacent cells for over a year, yet never once have I been disturbed by his early-morning rising.

You could say he is one of the old school, one who knows how to conduct himself in jail. He's done a lot of time over the past three decades. But he never complains and never bothers anybody. 'It's my own fault I'm in here,' he says whenever his recategorization or parole knock-backs crop up in conversation.

'Let's face it,' he is fond of saying as we sit together in Big Rinty's cell, trying to deconstruct the system over a jug of coffee, 'would you take a chance on a man with a history like mine?' But Felix is asking the wrong people. Unlike the authorities, when a prisoner looks upon a fellow prisoner he sees the man first, not necessarily the history.

Felix presents a cool character, calm and steady. But he wasn't always that way. Once, during an earlier sentence, a prison psychiatrist told him that he had 'the mind of the mad monkey: you want to be somewhere else, you want to be doing something else and you want to be somebody else.'

'So what's the cure?' Felix asked.

'There is no cure,' said the doc.

It was soon after that interview, some eighteen years ago, that Felix formulated his own cure. After plaiting strips torn from a sheet into a sturdy rope, he climbed on to his metal bed-end and tied one end of the cord to a crossbar on the cell window. Moments later he slipped a crudely fashioned noose over his head, drew up the slack so it was tight against his throat, and prepared to step out into space.

Twelve times that night Felix climbed on to the bed end and pulled the noose tight, until finally the crisis was over. 'On the twelfth time, I actually took one foot off the bed end and it was in that instant that I realized I had a choice,' he told me a few months ago, when we were talking about the different ways people cope with the prospect of long years in prison. 'So I made the choice to do the time. After that I felt in control, no longer helpless.'

After the night of the twelve noose tightenings, Felix never looked back. Buddhism beckoned, along with the Open University. And so he developed his still conspicuous philosophical outlook on life, death and the universe.

Clearly the new approach did not result in the resolution of all his troubles, otherwise he would not have spent so many years in prison. But the human psyche is complex and mysterious, and Felix is not without contrition for his past criminal actions.

Some people outside think that prison life is an easy option: no responsibilities, plenty of 'mates' with whom to play pool and darts and watch television. Some prisoners, it has to be said, think that way too – but not prisoners like Felix. At least, not until recently.

Countless years in prison are bound to take their toll on the well-being of even the most resilient character. When Big Rinty snapped at me last month, for example, I didn't really take it to heart. There was a bit of an atmosphere between us for a while, but when the big man tried to apologize a couple of weeks later I stopped him in his tracks. 'Shhht,' I said. 'It doesn't matter. You're stressed. You're entitled to the odd psychotic moment.' Then we laughed and shook hands.

It's different for Felix. He has reached a stage where all avenues forward appear to be blocked. According to the experts there is no more room on the scale for his risk factors. Probation, psychology and the Home Office are building formidable barricades between him and eventual liberty. The only hope lies in yet more offending-behaviour courses. But it's a long shot.

'My file must be that deep,' Felix said the other day, holding his hands out in front of him a couple of vertical feet apart. 'It's all been said. I've been analysed until I'm paralysed. And anyway, what do I want to get out for? Everything I need is in here.'

Rinty and I exchanged a glance. These words were not spoken in jest. We couldn't say anything at the time – he would not have listened. But I'm saying it now. Dig deep, Felix. 'Doing the time' was the right choice when things last got so critical. Spend longer considering your options. There has to be more to this existence than a life inside.

12 April 2001

A wind-up gives Bob a new name

Bob 'the true snake' has got a new nickname. Though it's true that he can be uncharitable sometimes, Bob's never really been a snake. He earned that nickname last year when Johnny Beggs got his transfer across to the enhanced wing after the two of them had fallen out over the landing newspaper. The tiff had still not been sorted out by the time Beggsy moved, and Bob was furious that Beggsy got to the luxury wing before him.

For the next couple of weeks Bob's criticisms became increasingly vociferous. Beggsy had only got a place on the enhanced wing, according to Bob, because he was 'a snake, a grass, and a blue-eyed boy'. But within a month of Beggsy's move, Bob's kit was packed and, with hardly a goodbye to anyone, he too had skedaddled over to the enhanced wing. Not only that, reports were soon emerging that the two men were to be found most evenings playing pool together and congratulating each other on good shots played.

Such hypocrisy could not be ignored. Which was why the lads Bob left behind on B Wing christened him 'the true snake'. I should add that this nickname is a secret, albeit an open one. The only person who to this day does not know it… is Bob.

I have always had time for Bob. He is a very easy person to do time with. In prison parlance he is what is known as 'a straight geezer': no previous convictions, obeys prison rules unquestioningly, and complies fully with all offending-behaviour course requirements. But that doesn't make him popular with everyone – hence the nickname, and more recently a particularly potent wind-up.

For the past few weeks Bob has been having his parole interview call-ups, which can be stressful if you're banking on parole, as he is. And lately Bob has had an extra stress factor to contend with, courtesy of his neighbour, Turtle – though nobody is supposed to know. (Baby-faced Turtle earned his nickname on account of his helmet haircut and protruberant Adam's apple.)

I tried to reassure Bob. 'From my experience of the system,' I told him, 'I'd say you have got a 70 per cent chance of a result. You've got no previous convictions,' I continued, 'you've never been nicked (placed on report), you've done the anger management, the victim empathy, and the enhanced thinking skills course. You're a prime candidate for parole – so long as you don't do anything stupid in the meantime.' But Bob had already done something stupid, Turtle told me (and anyone else he thought would appreciate a good giggle).

One day Bob was in Turtle's cell when he was struck by the image of a dark-haired beauty staring down from Turtle's picture board.

'Who's that?' Bob asked.

'My sister,' Turtle replied.

'Has she got a boyfriend?' enquired Bob.

'Not that I know of,' replied Turtle. Only it was all a scam. Turtle hasn't got a sister. The picture had been left in the cell by the previous occupant.

Bob asked if he could write to the beauty 'just as a friend'. 'Sure,' said Turtle, and Bob duly wrote a polite missive – adding reassuringly after signing off, 'PS, I am not a sex offender.'

Turtle was supposed to hand the letter out on a visit, but it never got further than the exercise yard, where all who saw it agreed it was a most entertaining read. The wheeze went further.

'Has she said anything yet?' asked Bob after a week with no reply.

Turtle paused for effect and then said, 'Er, only about the funny phone calls.'

'What funny phone calls?' said Bob.

'It's nothing,' said Turtle. 'She just thinks they're coming from the jail.'

Bob nearly burst a blood vessel. 'What!' he roared.

Turtle took a deep breath and said, 'She's going to complain to the governor if they don't stop.'

Suddenly relieved, Bob said, 'But they can get BT to check. Nobody here has got her number have they?'

Turtle was ready for him. 'It's my fault,' he said, looking at the ground and biting his lip. 'It was on a menu slip which I think I left by the phone.'

'Jesus H. Christ!' Bob exploded, no doubt envisaging allegations, perhaps further charges. 'There goes my (expletive deleted) parole!' Turtle recounted that bit well.

Though unaware of the fact, Bob has made a lot of people smile while he's been in here, and nobody begrudged him his year's parole when it came through last week. And most will say good luck to him when he goes home next month. No longer 'the true snake', but for ever remembered as 'Bob the stalker'.

26 April 2001

Why Ronnie came home

Nobody in here thought he was really going to go through with it. Open University student and Harry Potter lookalike Grebe was adamant from the moment the news broke that it was a hoax. 'It's got to be,' he said as the debate raged in the wing television room last weekend. 'Who in his right mind would willingly swap a sunshine paradise for a British prison cell?'

I didn't think there could be any argument about that. There can be few men in jail who have not wished on at least one occasion that the day would come when they could retire to a place abundant with sun and sand, teeming with scantily-clad babes – a place like Rio, for example. To contemplate the reverse of that would surely be unthinkable.

But it was no hoax. After thirty-five years as a fugitive, Ronnie Biggs at last returned this week to face the remainder of his thirty-year prison sentence handed down for his part in the so-called Great Train Robbery in 1963. Apparently he was hankering after 'a pint of warm beer in Margate'.

His return has generated lots of discussion in this prison, and no doubt in prisons up and down the country. And no wonder. While he was in Brazil, Biggs was the living embodiment of the prisoner's dream. He demonstrated not only that the system could be beat, but also that crime could pay and that it could confer on the perpetrator huge status and admiration. Biggs became perhaps the most potent anti-authority figure that this country has produced in modern times. A finer role model for those considering a life of crime would have been hard to find.

But not any more. When the private jet carrying the 'likeable rogue' touched down at Northolt airport that Monday, the fallacy of the Biggs legend was exposed forever. In here the collective reaction was tacit. As we watched the news footage of the jet landing and taxiing towards the police welcoming committee, everyone in the packed television room was united in silent disbelief.

Eventually Grebe spoke for everyone when he said in a half-whisper at the end of a deep sigh, 'Fucking hell…' Although he wasn't even born until five years after Biggs escaped from Wandsworth prison, Grebe understood fully the significance of the moment. For this was more than the mere return to custody of an 'unlawfully-at-large convict' (the official term for an escapee). This was history, our criminal heritage – previously only glimpsed in black and white via dog-eared photographs or grainy, hissing newsreel – being viewed first hand in living, breathing, twenty-first-century colour.

When the news ended the speculation began. Why? How could a free man voluntarily put himself in such a precarious situation? Biggs may not have enjoyed freedom in the true sense of the word while on the run but, compared to the confines of a prison, the freedom he did have was magnificent. That freedom was priceless. Yet he appears to have thrown it all away. Why?

In the television room explanations were rife. Grebe argued with Wicks. 'There's something going on here and we're not being told,' he said.

Wicks chuckled. 'There's nothing going on. Biggs just couldn't hack it any more.'

Grebe glared.

Big Rinty interrupted. 'Look, Biggs is an old man now. He's had three strokes for Christ's sake. Maybe he's skint. He might be back in jail, but at least he doesn't have to worry about health-care.'

'Are you kidding?' Grebe spluttered. 'Which jail have you been in where looking after prisoners' health has been a priority?'

Aldo piped up. (Aldo is about the same age as Biggs and has only had a half-dozen or so brief sorties from prison during the last forty-seven years.) He talked about the changes in the system since the sixties. 'In those days bread and water were routine punishment,' he said, 'and there were no talking on't exercise yard, and no radios in't cells.'

Wicks chipped in again. 'Ey, if Biggsy wants parole he'll have to address his offending behaviour! Mr Biggs,' he said, parodying the treatment administrator, 'we think you would benefit from the enhanced thinking skills course.'

Binker the Scouser interjected, rapier-like, 'He should have done that before getting on that fooken plane in Rio.'

The chuntering continued until finally it was Felix the Gambler's turn. 'Listen,' he said, panning the room with serious eyes, 'who knows what is in a man's head and a man's heart. Biggsy has made his decision. If he's at one with it, then that's all that matters.'

There was little anyone could add to that. But the debate is far from over. In the meantime, good luck Ronnie Biggs. You're going to need it if you're ever going to taste warm beer in Margate again.

10 May 2001

Skip learns a lesson

It sounded like a good deal, but it was obviously loaded: seventy-five phonecards for £100 cash (phonecards sell in the prison shop for £2 each). Deals like this are not too difficult to find in here, but I was surprised that it was Skip, a young lifer whom I've known for a few years, who told me about it one lunchtime last week as we walked together in the exercise yard.

'Hang on a minute,' I said. 'You've just done the ETS course and the parole board is reviewing your case for a move to an open jail. Do you really think it's wise to get involved?'

Skip has already been in closed conditions for several years longer than was stipulated in his sentence plan. More than once he has been shipped around the system under suspicion of this or that nefarious activity. Yet everybody who knows him on the landings knows he was just easily led and eager to impress.

It is nearly always the same when young men come to prison as teenagers. It is so much easier (and so much safer) to become a follower and hang with the crew. Skip was seventeen when he came in, now he's thirty. But his recent participation in the ETS course resulted in glowing reports from the tutors. So why was he involved with this dodgy deal? Not for the first time it made me question the relevance of offending-behaviour courses to the prison environment. I remembered my own experience on an ETS course.

'Can anyone define a problem for me?' The young female psychology graduate was standing next to a flip chart, upon which she had written in large red letters, 'Defining a Problem'. The ten of us who made up the ETS group had stared back at the young woman in silence.

'No? Very well,' she continued, and began writing and speaking at the same time. 'A problem... is the gap... between where you are... and where you want to be.' She rapped the full stop on to the board, making us jump, and then turned back to face us and added, 'Yes?'

Still our group remained silent. 'OK,' she began again, 'I want to go to the pub but I have got no money. Define the problem.'

Deaf Dave tilted his head so his good ear faced the front and flung up his hand.

'Yes?' said our tutor, pointing at Dave with her marker pen.

'You're skint!' said Dave, jubilantly. There were smiles among the group and somebody sniggered, causing Dave to scowl.

'No,' said the psychologist, firmly. 'Anyone else?' Save for the clearing of several throats, everyone stayed quiet.

'Right,' said our tutor and started to draw on the board again. 'The problem is the gap between where I am, i.e. "No money", and where I want to be, i.e. "in the pub drinking beer".' She ringed the phrases and connected them with a sweeping arc. Turning to face us again she asked, 'Now do you understand?'

Her smiling face deserved more of a response than another round of throat clearing and blank stares. But it was the first session of this newfangled course, and nobody really knew what was going on.

All that changed over the next twenty-odd sessions. The ten of us learned a whole new language. Problem solving became interesting and fun. A couple of prison officers assisted as tutors and we were set 'homework' to do in our cells at night. 'Using a CAF (consider all factors), a FIP (first important priorities) and a PMI (pluses, minuses, interesting bits), explain how you would organize and undertake a yeti-hunting expedition to the Himalayas.' Of course there were more serious aspects to the course and by the end of it most of us registered a significant improvement on the post-course questionnaires, indicating that our thinking skills had indeed been enhanced.

Back on the landings, however, it seemed that nothing had changed. Deaf Dave continued to cause grief to his neighbours

93

with his loud music, and Ropey still had to be escorted to the bath-house once a week and ordered to take a shower while everyone else was banged up. As far as I could see we just fell back into the same old routine and the same old habits, with too many years ahead of us to seriously consider yeti-hunting or anything else relevant to leading a normal life in the real world.

Now here was Skip having just done the course and, even on the verge of release, still prepared to tout a deal for one of the 'wheels' on the landings – or so I thought at first.

'You're going to laugh,' said Skip, 'but that's what I'm trying to tell you. When the geezer offered me five cards to broker the deal for him last night I told him straight. I said, "Leave me out, mate. I don't think like that no more."' Then he grinned and added, 'I think that course has really helped me.'

It was a sunny day and the birds were singing – and laughing was the furthest thing from my mind.

24 May 2001

How the home secretary inspired Todd

Some people may find this hard to believe, but I once saw a serving home secretary make a generous gesture to a prisoner. It seems like another era now, but in jail terms it was not such a long time ago: post the riot at Strangeways, but before the break-outs from Parkhurst and Whitemoor.

The prison where the home secretary's visit took place was a relatively small Victorian-built Category B. It was a place with high walls and heavily barred windows, yet despite its inauspicious appearance it enjoyed good relations with the local community. Its gym and education facilities were regularly made available to nearby schools for disabled kids, and the local press often ran reports of fundraising events organized jointly by staff and prisoners. This was a prison that prided itself on being a valuable community resource.

On the day of the home secretary's visit a group of prisoners, of whom I was one, was in a classroom with a teacher and a prison officer discussing last-minute details for the following weekend's sponsored half-marathon. Without warning, the classroom door opened and in strode the most powerful man in our lives, accompanied by an aide and two bodyguards (the latter were probably armed, or so we guessed from the strange hang of their jackets).

'Good afternoon,' boomed the minister (whose name is not important, but he did have a penchant for wearing brown suede shoes and smoking a large cigar with his pint). 'What's going on here, then?' The staff introduced themselves and explained our business. The minister seemed genuinely impressed.

'Seventy-eight laps around the prison football pitch?' he said, scrutinizing our motley group and emitting a throaty chuckle. 'Rather you than me.' We reflected his smile, lifted and encouraged. Several small-talk-filled minutes later, a nod from the aide signalled that the VIP visit was about to be brought to an end when suddenly a voice called out from within our group, 'Excuse me, sir.' Silence fell and all eyes turned towards Todd — nine and a half stone of skin and bones.

'Yes?' said the minister looking down with eyebrows raised at our frail comrade. An image of Oliver Twist in the workhouse refectory came to mind as Todd looked straight back and said, 'Can you give us a donation?' Glances were exchanged and breaths were held in the continued silence.

'A donation?' exclaimed the minister. But this was no Mr Bumble. Smiling broadly he reached into his jacket, pulled out his wallet, and extracted a crisp £5 note which he handed straight to Todd. 'There you go,' he said. 'Good luck with your run.' And then he and his entourage were gone. Once we had recovered from our collective gobsmack, everyone descended on Todd, congratulating and praising him for his initiative and courage. For what the home secretary did not know was that Todd was a chronic self-harmer who rarely spoke to anyone unless spoken to. He had been invited to join the fundraising group partly as a means of building his self-worth.

It is doubtful that the exchange with Todd even crossed the minister's mind on the day the run took place. But if he had enquired as to the performance of his sponsored runner he would have learned that Todd ran those seventy-eight laps as though his life depended on it. And when he finally crossed the finishing line he held his head up like a man who believed himself to be valuable. It was an incredible return for such a modest investment.

Sadly, Todd's benefactor was not to remain in office for long. We knew little about his successor, but we soon learned that he was not the sort of chap who would be inclined to hand over crisp £5 notes to jailbirds. Indeed, days as dark as night followed for those in prison. As political rhetoric turned to vitriol and vitriol to bile, finding a purpose beyond containment and punishment became a real struggle for prisoners. Voluntary constructive activities all but disappeared as difficult years were made even more so by the new champion of society's uncompromising attitude towards offenders.

There was some relief when, at last, the administration changed four years ago. The change was broadly welcomed. But the authorities have yet to establish a positively meaningful relationship between the state and those in prison. My message to whoever takes the helm at the Home Office for the next government is that such a relationship is essential if the prison system is to serve society properly.

I've seen with my own eyes what can be achieved with a little goodwill and encouragement. I saw it in Todd's face at the end of those seventy-eight laps.

7 June 2001

Cody has a bad day

When Cody got his 'Cat D' at the beginning of this year everybody thought that his troubles were over. This was a rare opportunity for a lifer 'in denial': being officially considered suitable for open conditions meant that he could be located on the enhanced wing, to wait for his transfer in the summer.

The day after he moved across, Felix the Gambler and I met him in the exercise yard. A normally effervescent character, we expected him to be even more ebullient now that he was living in comparative luxury. (Legend has it that the mattresses on those pine beds are a foot deep.) But mysteriously there was no sign of delight on Cody's bespectacled, sixty-eight-year-old face.

He noticed the two of us approaching, and before either of us could greet him he turned and, addressing us both, said absently, 'You know what? Last night I was in bed at half past eight and slept right through until half past six this morning.' There was a pause and then Felix shot me a look. Nodding wide-eyed at Cody, he said, 'Gooood.'

After another pause I nodded too and agreed. 'Gooood,' I said, 'that's good.' Our friend's demeanour had thrown us. We walked quietly together for a while and then Cody spoke again, 'That's the first time I've slept like that since I've been in prison.'

So that was it. Nothing was the matter. A good thing had happened, that was all. With our minds focused on Cody's dramatic change of circumstances we continued our walk in silence.

Prison life can be crazy sometimes. The livelier wings get nicknames like 'the Bronx' or 'Beirut'. To varying degrees everyone on the landing is vulnerable and a variety of defence mechanisms are manifest. Some prisoners exhibit 'psycho eyes' to keep predators at bay. Others talk loud and swagger, or walk around looking like they're carrying invisible rolls of carpet under their arms. Cody's defence mechanism for twenty-three years had been his unbridled boisterousness. But on the much more civilized enhanced wing he no longer needed it and his defences were down. His quiescent mood said it all.

We didn't see too much of Cody over the following weeks. He had developed a bowel illness which kept him away from the exercise yard throughout the spring, and his job in the kitchen kept his days busy. The rest of the time he spent cocooned in pine–bed–and–television land – until two weeks ago, when he had another reversal of fortune.

First he was accused of stealing cheese from the kitchen cold room. When he was confronted he denied everything. 'OK,' said Cook, 'we'll search your locker.'

'In that case,' said Cody, 'I resign.'

That morning he had awoken with the symptoms of a cold. Back on the wing he asked an officer to phone healthcare and the officer obliged. 'Can Cody pick up some pills?' he enquired.

'Yes,' answered Nurse. But Cody's bad day was just about to get worse. In healthcare Cody thanked Nurse for the pills and asked if he could also have a draught of cough mixture. 'I'm sorry,' said Nurse, who must also have been having a bad day, 'but you'll have to go back and ask the officer to call me again.' Cody could not face another quarter of a mile trek, but J Wing is right next door to healthcare. Perhaps an officer there could help him, Cody thought. The gate was open so in he went. Trouble was, in the wing office somebody else was having a bad day.

'Excuse me,' said Cody after knocking at the office door.

'Get off this fucking wing now,' said the officer in charge.

'But…' said Cody.

'Now!' yelled the officer.

After a brief argument Cody left, deciding the cough mixture was not worth the hassle. But the J Wing officer had been rattled. He awarded Cody a 'strike' for entering his wing without authorization. A strike meant Cody lost his enhanced status, which meant he lost his place on the enhanced wing.

That night Cody was back on the Bronx. He could have appealed, except for the (ahem) cheese business. Nobody liked what happened, but then it got much worse. Last week his bowel problem deteriorated. He was rushed to the outside hospital for a major operation. The last we heard, he was unconscious in intensive care.

28 June 2001

True colours are hard to see in prison

Last week, at the reception hatch, I found myself standing behind a fellow prisoner who normally professed to be hostile to 'the system'. I'd often heard him ranting on the landings about one grievance or another. As I approached and saw the man, I expected there to be some kind of argument in progress. Instead, I discovered pleasantries were being exchanged.

A parcel had arrived for the man and he was pleading for it to be issued to him early. (He didn't want to wait until the official time on Saturday morning and queue up with everyone else.) 'Please, guv, please – just this once,' he entreated. Eventually, the officer relented. 'Go on then you scrote,' he said, by now grinning broadly, 'but don't broadcast it, or they'll all be down here grovelling.' The man gushed his thanks, picked up his parcel and scuttled away victoriously.

'Next,' said the officer, before turning to respond to a remark from his colleague in the back. 'I know,' he said, 'they're only nice to your face when they want something.'

As I walked back to my wing, I reflected on this comment. What he said was true, up to a point. Despite being under almost constant observation, people in prison rarely get the chance to show their true colours. Prisoners who appear angry and bitter can be difficult to deal with sometimes – but how much does that really say about their characters? Others may appear to be polite and cooperative, but is that genuine? In jail, ulterior motives abound. Honesty is an elusive quality. But just occasionally something happens which reveals the unambiguous truth about a man's character.

Take Sid, for example, an old acquaintance of mine in the high-security prison system. Sid was as good as any advert for the anti-authority con. His bitterness was compounded as he had just finished a nine-year sentence and was planning to give up a life of crime when he was offered 'one last job' by former cronies. The job turned out to be a set-up, a 'ready-eye', and Sid received an eleven-year sentence. As a consequence, his frustrations were acute and prison officers took the brunt. 'I wouldn't piss on one of them if they were on fire,' he told me and others many times – a sentiment which turned out to be deeply ironic.

One day there was a fire in the prison hospital where Sid worked as a cleaner. The smoke was so thick that evacuation had been unruly and frantic. Stranded and alone, Sid stumbled blindly down a stairwell where he came across an unconscious prison officer. Without hesitation, Sid grabbed hold of the man and dragged him to safety – an act which proved that whatever he said on the landings, when it came to the crunch, Sid's humanity was still intact.

By contrast, a few days ago, a prison officer followed a prisoner he suspected of drug dealing back to his cell from the visits hall. As soon as the man closed his cell door, the officer took a discreet peep through the spyhole. Sure enough the man was retrieving a concealed package. The officer unlocked the door, rushed in and grabbed the package. 'I'll have that!' he yelled triumphantly. But the dealer was quick too. He jumped on the officer and snatched the package back. They fell out on to the landing just as Peanut was walking by. The dealer had the officer in an arm lock.

'Press the alarm bell,' the officer told Peanut. But Peanut – Mr 'Yes guv, no guv, I've changed guv, help me get parole guv' – hesitated.

'That's a direct order!' shouted the struggling officer.

But Peanut's allegiance to the 'criminal code' was greater than his concern for the officer. Instead of pressing the bell, he just turned and walked away.

'You'll regret that!' the officer called after him. Moments later, reinforcements arrived anyway and nobody came to serious harm – no thanks to Peanut.

Afterwards, everybody expected the officer to make Peanut's life a misery. In fact, he chose not to bear a grudge. The next day he called Peanut to the office. 'There will be no recriminations,' he said. 'I understand the dilemma you faced, and the fear of being seen by your peers to be siding with the screws.' Just to show there really were no hard feelings, the officer even offered Peanut his hand – and the nervous prisoner shook it.

It was a magnanimous gesture, and it just goes to show that when it comes to revealing true colours in prison neither side is predictable.

12 July 2001

Cody sets out his priorities

You have to hand it to Cody. He spends three weeks drifting in and out of consciousness in the outside hospital's intensive care unit and as soon as he is moved to a regular ward to recover he telephones the prison and asks to be put through to the kitchen. I can just imagine the look that must have appeared on Cook's face when he answered the call at 6.40am.

'Hello, is that Cook?'

'Yes?'

'It's Cody here. That cheese. I never nicked it. All right?'

'Eh?'

'All right?'

'Er, yes, no, hang on a minute…'

No explanations. No goodbyes. Cody hangs up.

Apparently Cook was furious. Later that morning, while stirring a vat full of bubbling mixed-bean casserole in tomato and parsley sauce, he was heard to exclaim several times to no one in particular, 'The bloody cheek of that bugger!'

Granted, it can be galling when, even with the odds stacked against him, the underdog gets one over on you. But maybe Cody was not being cheeky. The circumstances in which the cheese went missing suggest that he might well have been entitled to feel aggrieved by what happened.

Cody loved his kitchen job. He had sole responsibility for slicing and arranging the cold food – ham, corned beef, cheese etc.

before it was loaded on to the distribution trolleys. He kept the workplace immaculate. His standard of work was exemplary. So why would he jeopardize such a valued position for the sake of a bit of cheese? His problem was the same one encountered by any prisoner who has a job that involves access to, or responsibility for, a 'commodity'. This type of job attracts serious pressure from fellow prisoners. The hospital orderly, for instance, has to deal with people asking for needles. The reception orderly is pestered to access stored personal property. Those who work in the clothing-exchange store are badgered to provide new kit. Servery workers fare the worst as they face demands for extra or larger portions three times a day, every day of the week. A refusal is guaranteed to offend, and would be tantamount to an invitation to conflict, 'What are you – a fucking screw?' Telling the supervising officer might seem like an option, but this would be the surest way to acquire a reputation as a grass.

No. The wisest, safest response when these situations occur is to look whoever it is that is doing the asking in the eye and say politely, 'I'm sorry, I can't give you (whatever it is they're after), but if you want to take it... well, that's up to you.' Older, experienced prisoners know this. Cody, for all his protestations of having been wrongfully convicted, is classic 'old bird'. No snitching. No siding with the authorities. Whenever requests for cheese were made by fellow kitchen workers, Cody's response was standard, 'It's not my cheese. It's a big firm. I can't give it to you, but if you wanna take it I ain't gonna stop you.' And they did. Cody tried to cover the shortfall by slicing thinner portions. It worked for a while. Then came the complaints. Cook was obliged to act. In fairness, Cook did warn Cody a couple of times, before the confrontation and the threat to search his locker.

But Cody is a proud man. In prison terms he is staunch but straight. He would not dream of stealing cheese or anything else from the kitchen. But neither would he try to explain the circumstances in which the cheese in question had gone missing. Why bother? You'd have to walk in his shoes in order to understand. And anyway, on the scale of the world's problems, what's a bit of cheese? Or a good job in the prison kitchens? So, on a matter of principle, Cody resigned – before he was sacked, of course.

It was no individual's fault that his difficulties were suddenly compounded by the unexpected series of events that followed, culminating in the almost fatal deterioration of his health. As Stu the Guru always used to remind us whenever it seemed that things were not going the way we would have liked, 'Life is many things, but rarely is it fair.'

We probably won't see Cody here again. Following the surgery, he needs medical facilities unavailable in this jail, and perhaps that's just as well. He could be a complainer, and he did go on a bit about being innocent and all. But we won't forget him: his indomitable character, his eternal optimism, that smile. Good luck Cody. Wherever you end up, we wish you peace.

26 July 2001

This is true. I had loads of books obtained for me.

The Ragged Trousered Philanthropists persuade me I need glasses – *excellent*

Reading books, not surprisingly, is one of the most popular pastimes in prison. Modern prison libraries cater for almost every taste in literature. And if a particular title is unavailable on the premises a prisoner can place a 'special order' with the librarian (always a civilian worker), who will relay the request to the local county library.

Certainly books have always been important to me in prison – especially at the beginning. Radio was fine: music, drama, documentaries, news. All brought comfort through the longest, darkest hours of isolation. But nothing can focus a restless mind like a good book.

I read a lot of fiction in those days: mysteries, thrillers, adventures. Then one day in the prison library I came across an oddly titled book with a caricature of several jolly fellows on the cover. It was a thick paperback, more than 600 pages long. A quick perusal of the foreword and preface told me that this was a more serious type of book than I was used to. But it must have been at a time when for some reason I felt that I needed to be learning more. So I signed for the book and, along with several pulp novels, took it back to my cell – where the first thing I did was to look up in my dictionary the meaning of the last word in the book's title: *The Ragged Trousered Philanthropists*, by Robert Tressell. I still didn't get it, however.

We were allowed one visit to the library each week then, every Saturday morning. Despite several attempts during my first week with the book, I never quite reached the end of the first chapter. I couldn't work out the story. Something about a group of building workers in the olden days. Though it read like fiction it seemed to have political undertones, matters which to me at the time appeared weighty and incomprehensible. Determined to persevere with it anyway, I signed for it again the following Saturday. But again I failed to advance. For three weeks of what was then a twenty-three-hour bang-up, that book kept me company like a smug and incommunicative cellmate. Until at last I gave in and placed it back on the library shelf where I had found it – unread and uncomprehended.

Within a couple of years I had begun to attend education classes and my reading habits became more structured. Guidance from tutors and discussions with fellow prisoner-students enabled me to make more discerning book choices. During the ensuing years my interests developed imperceptibly along with my thought processes. And then, at a point that I do not remember, I found that among my most treasured possessions I counted books.

Not until around four years ago did I notice the change in my eyes. I picked up the book I was reading at the time and immediately detected a fuzziness around the type. The one thing that a long-term prisoner fears more than any other is deterioration, and now here was the first real evidence of my decline. I chose to ignore it. Apart from a negligible irritation, it made no difference to my ability to read – for a while at least. Then it did. A bleary tiredness would develop in both eyes if I tried to read for more than half an hour. I read less and less.

Finally, a year ago I had an appointment with the visiting optician. 'You need reading glasses,' he said, after close scrutiny of my eyeballs. But still I resisted, unable to acknowledge even this minor frailty, until a few weeks ago when something quite uncanny happened.

I stuck my head around Big Rinty's cell door one day and there on his table lay a copy of *The Ragged Trousered Philanthropists*.

'Whose is that?' I asked the big Dundonian excitedly.

'Library. Special order,' he replied.

'Can I borrow it?' I said.

He said I could but that I had to return it as soon as possible. 'If it's late back I'm not paying the fine,' he said.

It had been a long time since I had held that book in my hands. But the intervening years had not been wasted. That night I struggled with the small print, but not with the ideas being conveyed by Mr Tressell. I discovered a wonderful tableau of working-class life in Victorian England – eminently readable and perfectly comprehensible.

Rinty was unimpressed by my reading pace, however. After receiving his second fine in as many weeks he issued his ultimatum, 'Accept it man, you're getting old. Either you get glasses or I want that book back. That's 80p I'm down already!' There were no other options. I ordered the specs, with smart frames paid for from prison wages. They arrived last week. What a relief.

9 August 2001

A new man on the spur brings back memories

Andy Greight arrived on the spur a few months ago. He was finishing off a three-year stretch. I wasn't around when he moved into the cell opposite mine. So on the evening he landed I took a cursory look at the name panel above his spyhole cover. No, I didn't know him.

But it was an unusual name, and for some reason it had a vague ring of familiarity about it. The next morning, Andy was in the breakfast queue: slightly built, early twenties, fair hair, big eyes. Nope, I couldn't say I knew him. Though once again that hazy notion of recognition.

Before the end of the week Andy and I had had a run-in. After tea on this particular day I went to make a phonecall and found the booth occupied. My turn came and I reached over and tapped the panel gently. Without moving the handset, Andy turned and looked at me.

'Time,' I mouthed. He turned away and continued chatting. Two minutes, three minutes into my ten-minute slot. I tapped with more emphasis. Still no acknowledgement. By the five-minute mark I was gritting my teeth. Maybe it was an emergency, a crisis. Well, he could have at least stuck his head out and explained. When he did exit I had three minutes left.

'Thanks,' I said, as he brushed past me.

'What?' he said.

'What do you mean "what?",' I said. 'You've just used up all my time.' I jabbed a finger at my name on the booking board.

'God, I'm sorry. I didn't realize... The booking thing... Sorry about that.'

'Prat,' I whispered, as I closed the booth door.

In fact, as the weeks passed, my thoughts of Andy as 'the phone fiend' diminished. He took a job as a wing cleaner. People warmed to his easy smile. He was helpful. (Dirty crockery in the recess? A polite reminder. Forgot to collect cell-cleaning materials? He'd put some by for you.) Our phone feud was soon for-gotten, but still I had the odd twinge of déjà vu whenever Andy was around.

One day I was talking to Yodle (yawns like a moose – in the television room, in the recess, on his way to work) and out of the blue he told me, 'Andy's brother's doing life.'

Suddenly it comes to me. I ask him, 'Do you know his name?'

'Yeah,' he says, 'it's Martin.'

In an instant, I was nine years back in time. A high-security Cat B prison. I am sitting against the wall in the segregation-block exercise yard, next to a slightly built, fair-haired, big-eyed young man. He's struggling with his life sentence. I appear to be coping. The lifer governor has asked me to 'go and have a chat'.

Martin Greight had made progress fast – at one stage he'd made Category C. We talked about his transfer to the lower-security jail. 'I didn't like it,' he said. 'We lived in dorms.'

We talked more. Eventually I ask him, 'So what went wrong?'

'It was terrible...' He falters, then begins to sob.

'Take your time,' I say. 'I'm not prying. But you've got to get yourself back on track.'

He sobs a little more and then just blurts it out. 'Two guys,' he says, 'I... I was raped.'

It was the first time he'd talked about it. He didn't want the authorities involved. He was ashamed, embarrassed. 'I'll work it out myself,' he said. But it explained why his prison performance had suddenly gone awry – the drugs, the self-harm – resulting in the move backwards and the extra years. We spoke now and then once he was out of the seg, but our conversations were never so deep. Time moved on and so did Martin. I never saw him again, but just occasionally the fleeting image of his terror crossed my mind.

And now I wondered if Andy knew. He would have been fourteen or fifteen when I first spoke to his older brother. Eight or nine when his brother had been sentenced. I asked him one day, 'How's Martin?'

'You know him?' he said. I nodded. 'He's just waiting to go to an open nick,' he continued. 'We're not that close. He's been away so long. The family are looking forward to him coming home though, especially mum.' I could see it in his eyes. He didn't know.

Andy's discharge date was two days ago. I decided I had to tell him about his brother before he left. He said his goodbyes to the lads before breakfast, and then I stepped into his now bare cell and pushed the door to. He smiled and offered me his hand.

'Andy,' I said. 'Listen, your brother...' I squeezed his hand tightly. 'He's very brave.' Andy's big eyes looked quizzical. 'No, really,' I said. 'Whatever he did, be proud of him for getting to the end of this thing. He's very, very brave.' I could feel my eyes welling, and turned away.

'Greight!' called the discharge officer.

Andy picked up his bags. 'Coming!' he replied, and bustled out of the cell. I stood and watched him swagger down the spur. He was beaming. Before disappearing he turned and called back to me, 'Good luck mate!'

I didn't reply. Back in my own cell I sat down and wiped my eyes.

23 August 2001

Waiting for the lock down

It was the sight of prison officers in wellington boots probing with gardening forks among the shrubberies in the landscaped areas of the prison grounds which gave the first indication that something untoward was going on. And what about those long, black-handled gizmos with small hoops on the end that two of the officers were sweeping over the ground ahead of their fork-wielding colleagues?

'Metal detectors!' called a voice from the back of the small group of us who were bunched against the bars of the window at the end of the twos landing. Metal detectors? The conjecture began immediately.

'A knife's missing from the kitchen,' said Wicks.

'Do you know that?' said Felix the Gambler.

'No,' replied Wicks, pointing out of the window, 'but it's got to be somink like that with all that lot going on.'

Felix just shook his head and said, 'Somink my arse.'

'Maybe a tool has gone missing from one of the workshops,' said Binch.

'Or from the works department,' offered Yodle.

Big Rinty thought a key might be missing. 'It's been a while since they've had to change the locks in this place,' he said, looking at Felix, who nodded approvingly.

'Whatever it is,' said the Gambler, pausing long enough to catch everyone's attention, 'what's the betting that there's going to be a lock down.'

The officers had been spotted searching the grounds moments before the lunchtime bang-up. If there was to be a lock down (when everyone in the jail, apart from key kitchen workers, gets locked in their cells until further notice), it was likely to be in the afternoon. The searching officers would have been visible from three- or four-dozen windows like the one we had been looking out of, so whoever was involved would already have gotten wind that it was 'on top'. The authorities would have to act fast if they were to have any hope of pinning down the perpetrators.

But to everyone's surprise the doors were unlocked for afternoon movement at 1.45 as usual and the regime continued uninterrupted for the rest of the day. It made for an uneasy atmosphere. Knowing but not knowing. Guessing, wondering, thinking. The searchers with the metal detectors had set the rumour mill into overdrive, yet not a single piece of official information was forthcoming.

That night, few people were under any illusions that the next day, Friday, would be anything other than a long day behind closed doors. But morning arrived and still no lock down. Now if there is one thing that is guaranteed to raise anxiety levels in prisoners it is uncertainty. Routine is everything. Soul-destroying sometimes, but simultaneously numbing and comforting. It is routine in a prison regime that creates the vacuum which ensures the most painless passage of time. Stasis can be a wonderful anaesthetic. It may feel like it's dragging sometimes, but then you wake up one morning and find a month, or a year, or more has passed in a blink of an eye.

By Friday night the jail had settled. It seemed that the omens had been wrong. Perhaps that was the plan, to lull us into a false sense of security; or was it just logistics? Whatever the case, the message arrived before unlock on Saturday morning. 'Listen up you lot.' It was a female voice: Mrs C. 'There's a meeting this morning, so breakfast will be late.'

Half the spur was probably still in bed. Most of the other half would, like me, have had ears pressed against cell doors, gleaning extra information from the tone of her voice. Did she sound regretful? Concerned? Reassuring even? Mrs C, our wing's only female officer, could be all of those in the right circumstances. But today she sounded cool and businesslike. A meeting? On a Saturday morning? A meeting my arse.

They let us out two at a time to collect breakfast an hour later than usual. I stopped at Rinty's door on my way back. 'You OK in there?' I whispered through the gap by the hinge. 'Aye,' he replied, jumping off his bed. 'Listen,' he continued. 'This meeting. I think it's about Yodle going into the office last night to complain because George turned the telly over halfway through *Emmerdale*.' Before I could implore him to get a grip, Mrs C had shooed me back to my cell.

A long day followed. No gym, no library, no exercise, no newspapers – no mail even, until late afternoon after the sniffer dogs (a pretty spaniel and a Weimaraner) had been and had a nosey in our cells. Happily it was all over by the time England kicked off against Germany. As soon as they unlocked us everybody packed into the main television room. The mood was manic: the sense of anticipation for the big match exacerbated by long hours behind closed doors. For the next hour and a half the chanting and cheering must have been audible in the local town three miles away.

Five goals to England and a goal to Germany later, somebody screamed hoarsely to more cheers, 'Lock down? *What... fackin'... lock down?'* They allowed us a few more minutes to expend the last of our exuberance and then it was time to file out and back to our cells – exhausted and yes, grateful for the night–time bang–up.

We still don't know what the lock down was all about. But there's been little speculation. All we're talking about now is the football.

6 September 2001

Cody, rats, and the news from New York

We really wanted to believe the rumour, but it sounded too good to be true. Where did it come from? Who heard it first? 'Two screws were overheard discussing it,' said one voice in the exercise yard. Me, Big Rinty and Felix the Gambler decided to reserve judgment. If it was true, and our friend Cody had had his case referred back to the Court of Appeal by the Criminal Cases Review Commission, we'd hear about it first hand soon enough.

We knew that Cody had recovered well from the life-saving surgery he had undergone a couple of months earlier – we'd got that from Global, the hospital orderly. And we knew he was only lodged in the hospital wing of a high-security prison because this jail did not have the post-op medical facilities that he needed. He hadn't lost his Cat D status, and in fact the Home Office had arranged to transfer him to an open prison as soon as he was strong enough to travel. We had got that from Ragby, the governor's tea boy. The only glimmer of hope was that the commission had invited a final response to their 'statement of reasons'. Cody was optimistic, incautiously so some might have

111

said. But, though many of us in here thought the world of him, nobody believed that anything else he had to say on the matter would change the CCRC's mind. Until now – maybe.

It gave us plenty to talk about over the weekend. But then something happened which relegated the topic of Cody to the back burner. It was Monday lunchtime and the wing residents had been summoned to the day room. The PO (Principal Officer) wanted to make an announcement.

'Rats!' he yelled, grabbing our attention immediately. He'd stalked into the room with shoulders back and dark eyes flashing. Our sudden silence startled him. 'No,' he continued, panning the room with an outstretched index finger, 'I don't mean you lot.' And then he smirked at his little joke.

Once we had stopped grinning disingenuously amongst ourselves, the PO explained further. There had been a dramatic increase in the jail's rat population. A family had moved in near our wing's entrance. Mrs C had had a late-night confrontation with a longtail as she left the building at the end of her shift. 'She fled,' said the PO, 'and she's not coming back until the problem's sorted.'

But nobody sniggered. Nobody sneered. For everybody remembered that when the authorities finally agreed to let Felix the Gambler out for his first 'rehabilitative' shopping trip they stipulated a two-man escort. Mrs C had thought this was ridiculous. 'I'd take him on my own,' she argued. And in the end she did. The notorious risk-taker took great pleasure in proving that this petite lady's faith in him had not been misplaced.

The PO said that prisoners throwing food scraps out of cell windows might be contributing to the rat problem. 'Anybody caught will face heavy penalties,' he assured us, bringing the meeting to an end. Rat jokes were having a good run – until the afternoon of Tuesday 11 September.

Big Rinty saw it live. One of his jobs is to set the video to record satellite movies for the wings. 'I just flicked on to the cable news at two o'clock and there it was, happening,' he told us later. Nobody could believe it. All evening the TV rooms were packed but silent. Those images. That horror. The plight of those people. Incredible. Our troubles puny in comparison.

The next day a Tannoy announcement stopped us in our tracks. 'Notice to staff. Notice to staff. The prison is now on security-level amber. Security level amber.' What the hell did that mean? Grebe read a memo upside-down on the office desk. It was a standard set of instructions for all government buildings in the event of a major threat to national security. 'Amber means "get ready" doesn't it?' said Rinty. 'Yes,' replied Felix, and then added ominously, 'but get ready for what?'

Days passed but it still felt like Tuesday. Each day the same news, the same pictures. The president. The prime minister. The talk here was of nothing else. Until Saturday, when Cody phoned the prison kitchen. The CCRC really had changed its view. After all those years of pleading his innocence he had been let out on bail pending a return to the Court of Appeal. He left a number and Felix called him. Another piece of unbelievable news. Cody at home, safe with his family. Felix passed on our good wishes.

20 September 2001

Open conditions

Thoughts of rehabilitation

There is a famously memorable scene in the multi-Oscar-nominated prison movie *The Shawshank Redemption* in which one of the lead characters, Red (played sublimely by Morgan Freeman), is sitting in front of a parole panel after serving forty years of a life sentence. The scene is especially powerful because we, the audience, have already seen Red sitting in that same chair in front of a similar panel in an earlier scene in which he had been applying for parole after serving thirty years.

When on the earlier occasion he was asked if he felt that he had been rehabilitated, Red did not hesitate. 'Oh yes, sir,' he assured them in his most compliant tone, his face a picture of remorse and humility. 'I can honestly say I am a changed man. God's honest truth. Absolutely rehabilitated.'

At that stage it is almost impossible for those watching not to sympathize with Red when his application form is returned, stamped 'rejected'. For one, thirty years spent in whichever prison, let alone one with a regime as brutal and dehumanizing as Shawshank's, is a tough penance by any stretch of the imagination. But, more importantly, the audience has by then seen the way of life that Red has been forced to endure for all those years, and marvelled at how he has adapted to it. By then we know what the parole panel does not: that Red has become a prince in his prison community – a master of jailcraft, noble and bold and proud of his position in the prisoner hierarchy as 'the man who can get you anything' – and we cannot help but respect him for it.

Ten years later it's a different story. Red has had a bellyful. No longer prepared to play the role of compliant con, he enters the parole panel's chamber with his head held high like the prince we know him to be. He sits down and this time when the panel asks whether he feels he has been rehabilitated, Red looks each of them in the eye and says, 'Well now, let me see. You know, I don't have any idea what that word means. To me it's just a made-up word, a politician's word. Rehabilitated? It's just a bull-shit word. And to tell you the truth I don't give a shit.'

How the audience love him for that. And how we smile when his application is stamped 'approved' and Red wins his freedom.

I thought about this sequence a little while ago, as I sat waiting for my own parole application interview after having served seventeen years – small potatoes compared to Red, I know. But the relevant issue is a similar one: the question of 'rehabilitation'. What exactly does that mean? Like Red I know the literal meaning. But I've heard it used and misused so many times that, to a certain extent, I am inclined to agree with Red's analysis.

That is not to say I have given up on the concept of rehabilitation. On the contrary, the longer I've been in prison the more passionately I have come to believe in it. Unfortunately, in this country at least, how to survive the experience remains the primary concern of the majority of people who come to prison, whether it be for twenty days, or twenty years.

Although the prisoner is not present when the board sits, the system here for parole applications in life-sentence cases is not so unlike the one faced by Red. The review can take up to nine months. During this time the prisoner is interviewed by a host of prison professionals from the departments of probation, psychology, education and chaplaincy; then by prison officers; and finally by a single member of the parole board (who, incidentally, will not sit on the actual board of the applicant). All prepare reports.

For the first formal review, such as my own, release is not an issue. Only the question of a move to open conditions is considered. This is so that there can be a period of testing in a situation where risk can be more realistically assessed. If the move is granted it means that society is ready to let a man take the first step towards regaining his life.

I had an hour with the parole board member. With his silver hair and kindly smile, he reminded me of a magistrate I had once stood in front of when I was ten years old. He asked me questions and we talked for a while. He was probing, but sensitive. And then my hour was up. Did he ask me if I felt I had been rehabilitated? No. Thankfully he did not. But he did shake my hand as I left the interview room and wished me 'good luck for the future'. I thought that was a good sign. All I'm waiting for now is the answer.

4 October 2001

The wait for open conditions continues

For a while now I have been cautiously anticipating recategorization to Category D, suitable for open conditions. If and when it happens, it will mean a major change in lifestyle. No more bang-up. That's the first thing that springs to mind.

The average time a prisoner spends locked in his cell has never really changed during my time inside: up to fourteen hours and longer on weekdays and up to seventeen at weekends in many jails. Staff shortages usually mean extra bang-up, as do staff training days and 'incidents' (knives going missing from kitchens, tools going missing from workshops, serious assaults, surprise ship-outs, cell barricades, hostage situations). Some people get used to it, some people do not. I don't think I ever have.

The idea of life without bang-up is almost too good to contemplate on the face of it. And intriguing. How do people in open prisons spend all that extra time unlocked? Exercise perhaps. Not the usual prison exercise, mind you, walking around and around a yard in endless circles. Some open prisons have acres of grounds, and I've heard that prisoners are allowed to roam and ramble virtually anywhere they want within the perimeters, between designated times, seven days a week. On the other hand, I've also heard that such establishments have a reputation for maximizing the time prisoners spend in 'purposeful activity' (I'm assuming this means work, education and such like). During one twelve-month period one place in particular was reputed to have averaged forty-seven hours a week of this normally elusive jail commodity. Now this, coupled with all that potential roaming and rambling, does seem like quite a daunting prospect – exhausting even. But hang on a minute; I mustn't get ahead of myself.

This is my first formal parole review. It began in February this year and I'm expecting the 'answer' (the parole board's recommendation and the home secretary's decision) any day now. Either it will be a positive one and I will get my Cat D, which will mean a transfer to an open prison as soon as a space becomes available; or it will be a knock-back, meaning I must stay in closed conditions to do 'further work' – offending-behaviour courses or treatment programmes – and wait for another review in twelve months' or two years' time.

'Be on the safe side and expect a twelve-month knock-back,' said Big Rinty the other week when we were discussing my prospects in the exercise yard.

'But I've done everything they've asked me to do and more,' I said.

'So had I back in 1990 when it was my first review,' he said. 'But look what happened: out of the blue, a two-year knock-back. And no work to do. They just didn't think I'd done long enough.'

It's true that decisions by the authorities can sometimes be hard to fathom. Rinty served his two extra years in a closed prison and then another two in an open prison; when he was released he had served almost twenty years.

Rinty and I first met in the high-security system in the mid-eighties. Rinty was already years ahead of me in his life sentence. When he moved on I never expected to see him again. So to meet him in this prison when I first arrived two and a half years ago was a shock. He told me the story. He had been out three years, then there was a dispute – and a trial. A jury decided that no offence had been committed. But Rinty was recalled to prison anyway. Four years later, he is still in a deep, black hole and no nearer to getting back out.

Oh we talk about it, though I don't really know how he manages to keep going. He's got heart, I'll give him that. To get your life back, make something of it, and then have it snatched away again must be hard, no matter what the circumstances. Rinty takes full responsibility for his predicament. 'I got complacent,' he told me ages ago. 'I forgot where I'd been for all those years. I didn't realize how vulnerable I was.' Is that possible? To forget twenty years in prison? 'Once you're out there,' explained Rinty, 'you're just so happy to be free again. The last thing you want to be dwelling on is jail.' That was clearly his big mistake. It is a lesson that he has had to learn the hard way, in order to impart its message to me. If I do get my Cat D it will be difficult to leave the big Dundonian behind.

In the meantime I'll remain calm and circumspect. Every case is different. I know my own situation. I feel that I am as ready as I'll ever be to face the challenges that life in an open prison will present. I only hope the official view concurs with mine and not Rinty's.

18 October 2001

The parole review board decision arrives

The principal prison officer opened the briefcase on his desk and took out a packet of slim cigars. From where I sat he appeared grim-faced, but I had learned over time that his often blunt manner was not necessarily a true reflection of his mood or attitude towards the person he was speaking to. I had been summoned to his small, untidy office to discuss aspects of the report he was preparing for my first formal parole review. There were several questions he wanted to ask me before setting down his conclusions.

He drew a cigar from the pack and before lighting up he looked at me through dark, glinting eyes and said, 'Let me tell you something. When I first started this job twenty-seven years

121

ago I didn't like prisoners.' (At the time of this first meeting he had been my wing manager for a year and a half. I did not know him that well, but well enough to know that he was no hard-liner. I wondered if it was time, or something else that had changed him.) He explained that he had begun his career in a young offenders institution, a borstal, as such places were known in those days. Those in his custody were 'hooligans and car thieves, burglars and muggers,' and that was how he saw them. As far as he was concerned they had been put away to be taught a lesson and he would not hesitate to 'nick' anyone (place them on report for governors' adjudication, which could result in loss of privileges, loss of remission, or cell confinement) for even the slightest infringement of the rules.

His relationship with the young offenders became increasingly fraught, with each seeing the other as the enemy; and then things came to a head. One night the young officer (at twenty-one, barely older than many of his charges) was on night patrol. He entered a blacked-out dormitory and, as he trod silently between the two rows of beds, his torch light failed to pick out the trap. With a sudden snap, several lengths of twine laid across the floor were pulled tight and raised to shin height. The startled officer was tripped and toppled, causing an explosion of banshee-like laughter from his young antagonists, who quickly disappeared underneath bedcovers, ensuring no nickings.

A week later, the PO-to-be got his own back. Wielding two galvanized dustbin lids, he crept into the dorm in the early hours and began crashing lids together like giant cymbals, crying 'Laugh now, you young men without fathers!' or words to that effect.

The change came soon afterwards. He told me that part of his job was to supervise prisoner work parties in the local forest. 'It was an old PO in charge who brought it home to me,' he explained. 'One day he pulled me to one side and said, "Listen. If one of these trees fell on me these lads would do their damnedest to get it off me. But if it fell on you... well, they'd leave you to it. If you want to get something out of this job, see the person first, not the crime." It was the best advice I ever got.'

When I heard this story I too felt grateful to that old PO. For one of the most important jobs for those who work in prisons is risk assessment. It is a skilled task which requires confidence as well as circumspection, and would be meaningless if all the report writer saw when interviewing a prisoner was a crime label.

Of course, as a prisoner you can never know what is really going on inside an interviewer's head. The interviews for my parole application were completed and submitted to the parole board in June, and since then I have been waiting for the answer. There were just two options for the parole board to choose: stay in closed conditions, or transfer to open conditions. My answer came back last week.

I had been helping out in reception when the PO came in. 'Mornin',' he said as he marched past, straight into the office. When he came out I was having a cup of tea with Theo the regular orderly.

'Can I have a word?' said the PO, beckoning me to follow him into the property store. Once inside, he closed the door.

'What is it?' I asked, feeling a little anxious.

'Bad news,' replied the PO, offering me his hand, which I clasped. Possible bad-news events began to flash through my mind in preparation.

'We're losing you,' he said. 'You got your Cat D.'

My whole body felt as if it had been anaesthetized. Through a haze I could see the PO was smiling – an arrested moment in time.

'All right?' he said. I was still shaking his hand. He was pleased for me. I could see it in his face, in his luminous dark eyes. And I knew that he was shaking hands with the person first.

'Yes,' I answered finally. 'Thank you.'

1 November 2001

123

Learning to live with the knock-backs

It took a while for me to come down after receiving the news that I was now a Category D prisoner, the lowest security rating in the prison system. I had been careful not to hope too much. Not to expect. I had prepared myself for the knock-back, had it come. Too often I have seen people go into parole reviews knowing they were going to get 'a result' – only to see them struggle pitifully afterwards when the result turned out not to be the one they were expecting.

'Knock-back' is a term a lifer adds to his vocabulary early on in his sentence. And if he has any sense he will learn to respect it. When I began this journey, the practice was that a review known as an F75 would take place three or four years after the prisoner had been taken into custody. Reports would be prepared and submitted to the 'lifer unit' at the Home Office. When the F75 review was completed, usually within eight weeks, the lifer unit would inform the prison of the date at which the prisoner's case would be reviewed for the first time by the parole board. If, for example, it was decided this would take place six years after the first F75 review, that information would be given to the prisoner by a 'governor grade' (formerly assistant governor) during a 'call-up' (a summons to the office). The prisoner would then translate this into the common parlance for the inevitable exchange which would follow with his associates on the wing. Thus, when asked 'How did you get on?', he would reply, 'I got a six-year knock-back.'

There were three of us on a governor's call-up on the day I got my first knock-back. Our names were on the noticeboard when we returned from morning labour. I do not recall the name of the first to tap on the office door and go in – only that when he came out he was grinning from ear to ear. His black hair was cropped close to his scalp and two front teeth were missing. 'Five years,' he said to me and Rake, a stocky, red-haired Glaswegian, who was the other anticipant.

I was next. I had already served four years. I knocked and entered. The governor grade wore a tweed jacket over a green shirt and salmon tie, and peered at me through large brown-framed glasses. He reminded me of an RE teacher. 'Sit down,' he said softly.

I have no memory of him giving me permission to leave, but the next thing I knew I was stepping out of his office and closing the door behind me. Rake was tugging at my arm, but I was too numb to speak. As I made my way down the landing all I could think about was that number. I banged myself up and sat on the edge of my bed.

A short time later Rake knocked on the cell door and called my name. 'What's up?' I called back. He knocked again and pushed aside the spyhole cover. When I got to the door I could see that his eye was red and glistening, and a tear track ran down the side of his nose.

'What's up?' I repeated.

'Nine years,' he said. Then again, 'Nine fucken years.'

I didn't know what to say. Should I tell him about my thirteen-year knock-back? I couldn't bring myself to acknowledge it. 'Listen,' I said, 'don't try to look ahead. Just think of today, this week. Nothing has changed.' The words were as much for me as they were for him.

And now those thirteen years have passed. Once I had taken in the news of my Category D, things happened quickly. I told my pals Big Rinty and Felix first. 'But let's keep it quiet,' I said. One of my neighbours, Silver, had been waiting for his answer from the parole board for longer than I had and I wasn't sure how he would react to me getting the news first. Silver has been in prison since 1974 and has so far had four parole reviews – each one ending in a knock-back.

I knew he was anxious about this one and I did not want to add to his anxiety, but a couple of days later I was told that now I was a D Cat I had to move to the enhanced wing. Silver would be even more hurt if he found out before I told him.

His door was wide open, an Elvis tape playing at full belt.

'Silver,' I called, 'Can I have a word?' He turned down the volume. I took a deep breath and said it. 'I got my Cat D.' I was so relieved when he shook my hand. 'You should have got yours by now,' I said. 'You've been in too long.'

'Don't worry about me,' he said. 'It's me own fault. I'm too stubborn. I wanted to do it my way.'

I suppose, in the end, we all do it our own way. All that we can do is hope that we're doing it the right way.

15 November 2001

The enhanced wing

So this is how the other half live? Well, not the other half exactly. Only forty places are available on the enhanced wing, out of the prison's total CNA (certified normal accommodation) of 650. Maybe that's why I feel so uneasy about being here. Somehow it doesn't seem fair. 'It's not about "fair",' said the PO when I mentioned this while querying whether it was obligatory that I should move over to the enhanced wing. 'It's all part of the normalization process,' he added. 'You're a Cat D now. You've got to get used to the idea of living with fewer restrictions.'

I didn't think that would take me long, with or without the enhanced wing. But eventually I agreed that it was important to get a sense of moving on, of 'progressing'. After all, I had no idea how long it would take to get a transfer to an open prison. Why not enjoy a little 'normalization' in the meantime?

The actual move did not take long. Theo, the reception orderly, gave me a hand. He pushed the handcart the 200 yards or so while I walked alongside, steadying my several boxes of stuff – books and papers, mostly – some of which had accompanied me since the earliest days of my sentence.

There had been no goodbyes to say – not yet. I'd still be seeing the familiar faces in the exercise yard, at work, in the gym. In fact I wondered how different life would really feel on the enhanced wing. For all the alleged advantages, it was still confined, like the other six wings, inside the twenty-foot, steel-clad, razor-wire-topped perimeter fence. But now that I'm here I can attest that different it certainly is.

Moving on to the wing was like moving into a small prefabricated motel. Somebody said it was the same type of accommodation as that provided for the workers on offshore oil rigs – and that figured. The wooden-slatted building is divided into two floors, each with twenty living units set in two rows of ten separated by a narrow corridor (not unlike the standard-class cabins section on a cruise liner, I imagine). The pristine white melamine-walled rooms are soundproofed, and each has a large unbarred window, as well as (I'm almost ashamed to report) mains electricity, a colour television, hot and cold running water, and an en-suite toilet and shower.

The Scandinavian pine beds are a good deal roomier than the standard steel prison cot. The mattresses, while not quite a foot deep as rumoured around the rest of the jail, are soft and sleep-inducing. Even though I've been in here for over a week, it still feels like I've been sprung from prison and I'm in a 'safe house', waiting for the next stage of the escapade.

The joke among the prison officers when talking about this wing is, 'I've paid good money to stay in worse hotels.' And many people outside would be outraged to see prisoners living in such relative luxury. Others, however, would say that the loss of liberty and being kept away from family and friends is sufficient punishment. They would argue that physical as well as psychological deprivations serve only to foster further resentment in many of those incarcerated, potentially creating worse problems for society when they are released. My view lies somewhere in between, though I must admit – despite the lack of the stress and pressures associated with life on a 'normal' wing – I'm finding it difficult to relax in such embarrassing comfort.

Perhaps it's the conditioning. I remember once trying to explain to an SO (a rank below PO) that imprisonment as I was experiencing it was debilitating, depersonalizing, dehumanizing and… 'Now hang on a minute,' he said before I could finish. I sensed that he was offended. 'It's not a criticism,' I said, 'just an observation.' I added, 'And let me assure you, I wouldn't have it any other way.'

But I knew he didn't understand, especially as, at the time, we were on a brand-new wing that had cost £8m to build – complete with pink walls 'to reduce levels of aggression amongst the inmates' (which failed, by the way). The point was – and still is – that, for me, overcoming the difficulties and negative aspects of prison life had become a valuable character-building exercise. That is why this 'luxury' feels so disagreeable.

But not for much longer. They told me a couple of days ago that my movement order had arrived and that I'd be going to an open prison next week. At last, after seventeen years, a chance to test this new character. This really is the beginning of the new beginning.

29 November 2001

It's farewell to Rinty and Felix – and a surprise in open conditions

'Be ready for a culture shock,' said Big Rinty when I told him and Felix the Gambler about the movement order and that I was going to an open prison on the next available Group 4 wagon. Felix concurred. 'Big culture shock,' he said. I didn't want them to think that I was being blasé about it, but I was sure that I would take it all in my stride. After all, this move was something that I had spent years preparing for.

There had been no guarantee that I would get a Cat D when my case was reviewed by the parole board earlier this year, but I had cautiously anticipated the result. When it came there was no real sense of joy, or excitement; just relief and gratitude that my efforts had been acknowledged. My couple of weeks on the enhanced wing had been like a period of rest and recuperation, a chance to collect my thoughts and get ready for the challenges that lay ahead.

Once in open conditions I expected few surprises. I had imagined a period of acclimatization, then perhaps a programme of gradual reintegration into the outside world; possibly community work to begin with, then perhaps town visits – and maybe eventually the opportunity to look for paid employment. Going by what I had heard on the grapevine, that appeared to be the normal procedure. I didn't expect any of it to be easy, but it seemed a heck of a lot more logical than much of what I had already experienced in the closed system. Nevertheless, there was something else waiting for me here at the open jail, something that I could never have anticipated and would not have known how to prepare for.

Leaving the closed prison was not difficult, though I dreaded saying my goodbyes to Rinty and Felix. That was why I left it to the very last minute. Felix made it easier for me. He was standing outside the main entrance to my old wing talking to Yodle as I approached. As soon as he saw me, he turned and disappeared inside. At first I thought he had nipped in to Rinty's cell so they could say their goodbyes together. But when I got there Rinty was alone.

His cell door was ajar and the big Dundonian was sitting at his table arranging his library books into strict reading order (and woe betide anyone who touches them once they've been 'organized'). I knocked at the door and entered.

'Where's Felix?' I said.

'On the blower,' said Rinty.

'Well that's it, Big Yin,' I said. 'I'm off.' I offered my hand and the big man took it and squeezed hard.

'Good luck,' he said. I tried to reciprocate the sentiment, but the lump in my throat wouldn't allow it. And anyway, Rinty needed more than luck.

'I'll write,' I said, and quickly left the cell.

When I got to the phone booth Felix had the handset pressed against his face. I bent down and caught his eye. 'I'm going,' I mouthed. Without moving the handset, he nodded his head and thrust out a hand. I took it in both of mine and held tight. 'Take care,' I said, and then turned and hurried away from the wing; there was no sense in prolonging this strange pain.

Just a few days earlier, Felix had handed the wing PO a letter informing the authorities that he no longer wished to be considered for release. He'd had enough of what he considered to be a pointless game, he explained when he talked it over with me and Rinty beforehand. 'Gold stars,' he said. 'That's all I'm ever going to get from doing their offending-behaviour courses. I could run them myself, I've done so many.' We both thought his letter was an extreme move, but he hadn't taken the decision lightly. 'I feel I've lived my life,' he said, 'and that's all there is to it.'

I thought about all of this and so much more as the Group 4 prisoner-transit wagon ferried me along to my new location. I was the only prisoner on board which meant the journey was an unusually quiet one. I didn't think too much about what lay ahead as I gazed out of the cubicle window at the free world in action. It was pointless to speculate about unknown territory.

Two and a half hours later the prison came into view from a distance of about a mile. It was set high on a hill and looked more like a farm then a jail, except for the fence – but there was no razor wire on top, and no steel cladding below. Moments later the entrance gates were opened by an OSG (an operational support group worker, not quite a prison officer) and the Group 4 wagon pulled in and drove around to a small courtyard. A sign by the side of an open door read 'Reception'.

The two Group 4 men unloaded my bags of kit and handed me over to a prison officer who signed for me as if I was a registered package. 'OK,' he said, handing back the clipboard. 'All in order.' A couple of minutes later the gate was opened again and the wagon drove away into the darkness. This was it.

The reception process was informal. Just two prison officers, disarmingly helpful and friendly; and I noticed there was no prisoner 'reception orderly'. My kit was checked speedily and then, confusingly, the prison officers picked up a bag of my kit each. The one with the moustache noted my look of puzzlement and smiled, first at me then at his colleague. 'Follow us,' he said. 'We'll show you to your room.'

This helpful attitude was totally alien to any other reception process I'd ever encountered before. And then there was a bigger surprise. Just as I picked up my last bag of kit to follow the officers, a man with a clipped moustache and a military bearing, dressed in jersey and slacks, stepped forward and introduced himself as the prison's probation officer. He offered me his hand and as I shook it he delivered his thunderbolt. 'Welcome,' he said. And then he said it again, 'Welcome.' The warmth and conviction in his voice was overwhelming.

'Thank, you,' I replied, trying for the second time that day to check the constriction swelling in my throat. My pals were right after all. There really was more to this 'open conditions' situation than I had bargained for.

13 December 2001

A face from the past shows me the ropes

The last time I saw Mickey Folsom he had looked haggard and old. I didn't know much about him, only that he was a minor London 'face' and that he was transparently staunch (strictly no grassing and no 'having it' with screws or nonces).

At the time we were in a small Victorian model prison in the Midlands which had just the one wing holding 200 prisoners. His cell was at one end on the twos and mine was at the other on the fours, so we spoke infrequently. But from the odd conversation we did have – usually when we bumped into each other in the meal queue – I learned that he was five years into a twenty and that without parole he was looking at another eight and a half years inside before his EDR (earliest date of release). I also learned that it wasn't the time he had done that had worn him down, but the thinking about the time in front of him. 'I'm never going to get through this,' I remember him saying more than once. 'It's just too long.'

Mickey was a short, dapper man and, though he was tiring under the weight of his sentence, even in prison clothes he was always immaculately turned out. I liked that about him, but he and I could never have been described as associates. In fact, when he was transferred I didn't notice he had gone until weeks afterwards when someone mentioned his name in passing. Funny then that, seven years later when I land here in open conditions, the first prisoner I meet (who also turns out to be my next-door neighbour) is Mickey Folsom. We greet each other like long-lost buddies.

When the handshaking and shoulder slapping is over, Mickey invites me into his room for a cup of tea. 'You're looking well,' I say eventually. I'm not lying. I think he actually looks younger than he did the last time I saw him, and I tell him so. 'It's this place,' he says, shaking his head. 'It's unbelievable. No stress, no pressure, no fackin' idiots.'

There's a knock at the door and it's Mickey's friend Del. Del is a jovial, heavy-set man in his fifties with a mop of jet-black hair that doesn't appear to match his lived-in face. Mickey introduces us. 'We was in the B Cats together,' he tells Del, who smiles and grasps my hand firmly. I wince inside at Mickey's intimation that he and I were friends back then. But what does it matter? It is good to meet a familiar face. And there really is a certain affinity that grows among long-term prisoners the further down the line they get, so long as they keep their heads, that is.

Mickey has certainly kept his head. He only arrived here seven months before me but already he's working for a private company as an industrial cleaner. He and Del work together. They are picked up in a van at the gate every evening at six and are brought back at around four in the morning. The work is dirty and hard, but they earn a real wage, most of which is saved for their ultimate release.

At first, my conversations with Mickey and Del in the dining hall seemed surreal. But listening to this once abrasive and anxious man as he talks to his friend about shifts and travelling time and plans for a normal, crime-free future is heart-warming and inspiring.

Mickey helped me to settle in by showing me around. 'The main thing about this place,' he said, 'is that you've got to get used to thinking for yourself.' He showed me the 'canteen' (prison shop) and explained the procedure for making purchases. He took me on a tour and told me which parts of the grounds were out of bounds. I commented that there were few prison officers around. 'That's the point,' he said. 'You're not expected to need supervising.'

Well that sounded easy enough. Three days later I find myself standing in the doorway that leads out on to the sports field. I've got myself a little daily cleaning job, just a corridor and a couple of toilets, but once it's done, my time is my own. I'm dying to go out and walk, but... Then Mickey arrives.

'What's up?' he says, but he can see it in my face. 'Go on,' he urges, 'get out there. You don't have to wait for permission.'

Every day now I go out walking, in the rain, in the dark. I can stay outside until 8pm if I want to. Every day now it feels like Christmas. I'm still here, still a prisoner – but no longer a captive it seems. Happy New Year.

10 January 2002

Neither bitter nor broken

Cynical prison officers will tell you, 'Everybody in prison is innocent.' But while it is true that many prisoners, particularly those serving long sentences for serious crimes, protest their innocence, few sustain that position for very long. Most buckle down after a year or two, accept their guilt, and get on with the task of coming to terms with their crime and serving their time. Those who continue to 'fight their case' have to be prepared for

133

years of the most intense frustration and mental anguish, without ever knowing when, or even if, it will ever come to an end.

And if such a person who was finally cleared by the Court of Appeal should happen to express a measure of bitterness towards the police, the system and British justice, who would blame them? Who could? It would be perfectly understandable to anyone on the outside, after all. The longer a victim of a miscarriage of justice spends in jail, the more bitter most people would expect that person to be. Which makes Stephen Downing's obvious lack of bitterness after enduring twenty-seven years of wrongful imprisonment all the more remarkable.

I listened to Stephen as he was being interviewed on the *Today* programme yesterday morning and was struck by how dignified he remained in spite of the interviewer's gentle but determined probing. He was not angry at the police. 'It was a different police force. Most of those involved in my case are now dead. All that's in the past now. We have to move on.'

No matter how much the interviewer tried to coax him, Stephen clearly had no wish to express any resentment or apportion any blame. Neither did he wish to discuss the issue of compensation, only doing so briefly and courteously in response to the interviewer's persistence. 'All I would really like is a nice car and a comfortable place to live.' It was at this point that it occurred to me that his conduct, given the circumstances, was almost statesmanlike.

Having lived on the landings in the same prison as Stephen for a while, however, I should not have been surprised by his demeanour on the radio. In the outside world he appears to conduct himself no differently to how he conducted himself in jail: with unerring dignity and self-respect.

When I came to prison, Stephen had already served more than ten years, but it was another ten years before I heard his name mentioned, and several more before I actually met him. A friend of Stephen's had asked me to pass on his regards when he found out I was being transferred to the jail that Stephen was in, so within days of my arrival I made enquiries. I learned that

Stephen was one of the best-known prisoners in the place. Not because of anything to do with his case, however — nothing to do with any protestations of innocence — but because he was the longest-serving listener in the prison. Eventually he became the listener coordinator, a full-time post that meant he was on call twenty-four hours a day for those in distress. This was a position of the utmost trust and responsibility, requiring a person who possessed compassion and patience in abundance. How ironic, then, that it should go to a man who, in theory, should have had the most difficulty in coping with his predicament.

I spoke to Stephen often during the time that we were in the same prison. I could not claim to know him well, but well enough to find it hard, if not impossible, to believe that he could ever have had anything to do with the crime for which he served twenty-seven years. I could not say exactly why that was, though perhaps it was partly because of his consistent selflessness and the fact that he seemed to be encased in a protective aura of self-belief.

So he is not bitter. Neither is he broken. If anything the experience has been so profound that it has added a unique depth to Stephen's character. But just because he has appeared so calm, well adjusted and forgiving since his release on bail last year — and even more so after the formal quashing of his conviction this week — nobody should be fooled into thinking that maybe he did not suffer greatly during his incarceration.

I know the dark places where Stephen spent those twenty-seven years — and so does Gerry Conlon of the Guildford Four, who said when he was released in October 1989 after serving fifteen years, 'If there is a hell, it is being in prison and knowing you are innocent.' This is something worth thinking about whenever we see or hear Stephen Downing and note his graciousness.

17 January 2002

In working clothes prisoners look just like everybody else

Years ago, I was in a jail where the prisoners produced a regular magazine. One issue had a comic illustration depicting a bald, sallow-skinned, wart-faced man wearing an arrow-patterned suit and staring wild-eyed from behind the bars of a cell window. The cartoon convict's exaggerated smile exposed large gaps where several of his front teeth should have been and the speech bubble hovering next to one of his cauliflower ears said, 'Come to prison – it's great!'

Most people who saw it smiled, and few missed the point (it was published during a particularly intense period of media out-pourings about the 'cushy' conditions enjoyed by those in British prisons). The picture also mocked the stereotypical image of prisoners which, until then, was not something I had spent much time thinking about.

Soon afterwards, the prison's visiting room was being refurbished and, along with several other prisoners, I volunteered to help paint the walls. Normally there were three or four men painting, overseen by a single prison officer. But on one particular day, when two outside contractors arrived to fit the carpets, only I had been available for work.

It was mid-morning by the time the contractors turned up. George, the escorting officer, let the men into the building where I was working, and moments later received a call on his radio to report immediately to one of the wings. 'I'll leave you here,' he said to me. 'You're locked in so you can't go anywhere. Put the kettle on if you like,' he added, and then winked. 'Keep your eye on those two buggers. I'll be back in ten minutes.'

The contractors were grateful for the offer of tea, and when it was ready I carried two steaming mugs over. The younger of the two asked how long I had been 'on the job'.

'Just a few days,' I said. 'There's usually more of us, but the others are on call-ups today.' They both nodded, though I realized that they probably had no idea that a 'call-up' was a parole or recategorization interview with a psychologist or probation officer. They were based in a town eighty miles away and told me that they had never set foot inside a prison before.

'What are they like?' asked the younger one, nodding over to the window, through which a broadside of the old Victorian main wing could be seen running parallel to the visiting building. I listened for the sound of George's keys before confiding in lowered tones, 'They're not too bad. Most just get on with what they have to do.'

'Do you get many troublemakers?' asked the older one. That seemed a funny question, but it was true, I suppose, that prison officers were often portrayed by the media in just as negative a light as prisoners. Before I could answer, the younger one said, 'Is there anybody in there we've heard of?'

This left me stumped. I tried in vain to think of the names of any prison officers who might be well known, or even just known, on the other side of the wall. 'Erm...' was as far as I got before the sound of George's keys jangling signalled his return. 'I'm sorry, I've got to get back to work,' I said. 'Ask George. He'll know of any famous ones.'

Ten minutes later I was rolling away with the paint, spreading 'county cream' to my heart's content, when the sound of George guffawing stopped me in mid-roll. I turned to see what the joke was but, whatever it was, it had clearly gone over the heads of the carpet fitters. Then I heard George, still laughing, say, 'He's a con...'

He's a con? Christ, I thought. It hadn't occurred to me that the contractors might think I wasn't a prisoner. I smiled and nodded in their direction but both looked away stony-faced. How my face burned as I finished the rest of that wall. George told me later that with me dressed in old jogging bottoms and a jumper, they had assumed that I was a civilian worker. Especially with him leaving them locked in alone with me.

That incident served as a powerful illustration of the preconceptions many on the outside have about those on the inside.

Since arriving in open conditions a few weeks ago I have thought about it often. Every day I see dozens of prisoners going out of the gate to work – real work – as a precursor to resettlement and, I suppose, rehabilitation. They dress in all manner of outfits: from suits and overcoats to bomber jackets and bobble hats. Some even carry briefcases. Oh – and I've looked carefully – there is not a single cartoon convict among them.

24 January 2002

Stevens does a runner

Precious opportunities abound in an open or resettlement prison such as this one. The freedom to come and go within the grounds as you please; the emphasis on personal responsibility; and the further education and vocational training leading to voluntary and eventually paid work in the outside community.

It's all such a far cry from the usually torpid and mostly destructive environments of many Category B and Category C prisons. When I arrived here at the end of last year it was like emerging from a long, dark tunnel. I like to think I served my time in the tunnel well, but the idea of having to go back does not bear thinking about. That was why it was so hard for me at first to figure out how Stevens, the man who lived in the room opposite mine, should fail to return to the jail after finishing his shift at a local factory a few days ago.

In spite of our close proximity it was a while after I landed before I actually laid eyes on Stevens. A sign on his door gave me a clue as to why he was so elusive. The sheet of A4, attached with a single drawing pin, was grubby and torn and the words were scribbled in black marker pen. 'Nightworker. Please be considerate.'

The message was self-explanatory. I knew Mickey Folsom was doing shiftwork, but for some unknown reason it hadn't occurred to me that such an arrangement might be possible for anyone who chose to do it. The idea was so alien to anything I had ever encountered in prison. When I asked Mickey about it later, he said, 'I told you. They come and go at all times of the day and night in this place.'

Mickey explained that Stevens worked five eight-hour shifts, leaving for work late in the evening and returning at dawn. It sounded like an eminently practical way to serve the latter part of a prison sentence. Work at night, sleep during the day, pay your taxes and save enough money so that the chances of successfully reintegrating into the outside world could be maximized. It was appealing. It would be some months before I would be eligible for paid work, but there was no harm in planning ahead. Maybe I could pick the man's brains, I thought.

In the hope of catching Stevens, I started to leave my door ajar in the afternoons so that I could peek out whenever I heard his door open. For the first week and a half, however, I only saw people going in. Not only that, the people I saw were always acting suspiciously: looking both ways and over a shoulder before stepping into the blacked-out room. More than once I had to hop back quickly to avoid being spotted. I began to feel like a curtain-twitcher.

Then we met. It was a weekend. He and I emerged from our rooms simultaneously and I nodded, 'Mornin'.' He blanked me. Perhaps he was tired. His peaked cap couldn't disguise the fact that he did not look well. His face was gaunt and the black rings around his eyes were accentuated by his corpse-like complexion. Not enough sleep?

We spoke briefly when he had some time off over Christmas. He passed me a newspaper. 'How do you find working nights?' I ventured. 'It's OK,' he said, then closed his door.

The furtive behaviour of his visitors became more noticeable. Eventually, over a cup of tea in Mickey's room, I broached the subject. 'Mickey,' I said, 'is there anything going on over there?'

He turned and faced me. 'What do you think?'

'I think he's on the gear,' I said. Mickey shrugged his shoulders. 'If he wants to be a mug in a place like this...'

It emerged that Stevens was known as a hard-drug user. Cynics said that he'd 'worked his ticket' in a closed prison by bluffing his way on to a drug-free wing, and becoming a 'peer counsellor'. What? So he could wangle his way to an open prison where the drugs are scarce, and find a job working five nights a week? Some ruse.

It was the MDT (mandatory drug test) he took last week that brought it on top for him. The urine samples are sent away for scientific analysis. They say Stevens knew the result would be positive – which would have meant an automatic return to closed conditions. As powerful an incentive as any not to come back from work that night, I suppose, though the time will have to be served in the end.

In a way he did the place a favour by absconding. But I can't help thinking he would have done himself a bigger one by staying and facing the music. His real failure was not the use of the drug, or even the breach of trust. His real failure to my mind was to squander a precious opportunity.

7 February 2002

Psychology students arrive for a tour of the prison

The senior officer was in the house office, sitting on the desk and swinging one leg when I arrived. The door was open. It was Friday morning.

'You wanted me, guv?' I said.

'Yes,' he said, looking up from a handful of paperwork. 'We've got some psychologists visiting the prison next week and I wondered if you would mind showing them around?'

'Me?' I said. 'But I've only been here two minutes.'

'So?' he countered. 'You know your way around, don't you?'

'Yes,' I said.

'Well then,' he replied.

Over the weekend, I decided that it was in fact a compliment to have been asked. A signal that I was no longer considered to be a 'new boy' in the jail. Though it did occur to me later that I should have asked the SO for more information. The obvious question, for example, was: how many psychologists would be coming? Since it was the SO's weekend off, it was too late to ask him. I'd just have to wait and see and play it by ear.

'A minibus-full!' It was Monday morning, and I was echoing the gate officer's reply to my query. I had anticipated three or four, but now it seemed that a full-blown platoon had arrived. Thankfully, I was not going to be alone. Buster, a fellow prisoner who had been in the jail a few weeks longer than me, had also been asked to be a guide – though neither of us knew about the other until that morning.

It turned out that there were nine young women – all students, it emerged, and none over twenty-five – and one middle-aged man in the party. They were waiting for us when we presented ourselves at the boardroom. We cleared our throats, and in unison said, 'Mornin'.' From their seats around the huge table, the visitors reciprocated, flashing an array of reassuring smiles. An older lady was finishing off a briefing and suggested that the party split in two for the tour. Buster and I agreed and a couple of minutes later, each with our group in tow, we were on our way.

The man, who explained that he was the tutor, was in my group – along with a blonde girl, one with plaits, a dark-skinned girl and a girl with long black hair. As we walked around the grounds, it struck me that they would barely have been out of infant school when I began my sentence. They were friendly, smiley and curious. Just before entering the main accommodation block, I asked them if it was the first time they had ever been in a prison.

'Oh no,' said the blonde girl cheerily, 'we were in Broadmoor the other week.'

'Mmm,' I replied.

For the next forty minutes or so we looked at the gym, the

library and the education block, all of which, they said, compared favourably with the facilities of their college campus. They asked lots of questions: yes, people could take paid employment outside the prison; no, there was no limit on visits from family and friends. It must have sounded like an attractive existence for, as we headed back to the boardroom, the dark-haired girl stopped and asked, 'Aren't you worried about getting out?' She smiled, a little nervously I thought. 'Not as worried as I am about being in,' I said, perhaps a tad smugly.

Viewed through their eyes, I could see that what had been presented was a seemingly pleasant environment where board, lodging and leisure facilities provided a secure lifestyle apparently free from the pressures of 'real life'. But it was certainly no holiday camp. It was important that they understood, I explained, that some men were unable to handle the responsibility and accountability that such a regime demanded. 'This is a resettlement prison,' I said, adding, 'it is in no way representative of the general prison system.'

On the other hand, I did not want to paint too bleak a picture of the system as a whole; after all, I had benefited greatly from my years in prison. Nevertheless, my view was that that was mainly down to me and not the system. The knowledge of what time inside can do to people – the knowledge that can only come from experience – made it necessary for me to make the point. 'Prison as it stands generally dehumanizes,' I said, 'but this place is designed to rehumanize.' The girl nodded her head.

The tour over, the man thanked me and we shook hands. As they walked back to the boardroom, smiling and waving in my direction, I recalled my reaction to the welcoming handshake I received from the prison probation officer the first evening I arrived here. For days afterwards, my eyes welled up every time I thought about it. It would take more than a forty-minute tour to understand that, I thought, as I waved back at the visitors.

21 February 2002

A day release conjures up memories of Felix

Getting back out into the outside world after a decade or two behind bars can be a tricky business. Last week I had my first taste of 'community work'. It was the refurbishment of a village hall: painting and decorating and rubbish clearing. There were five of us in the party – all dressed in a variety of boots, jeans, baggy tops, and jackets – including Taps, the supervising officer who drove us to the location in a people-carrier.

How could anyone have guessed that four of our number were still doing time? And that collectively we had so far served a total of forty-two years? To the untrained eye we must have looked like just another gang of jovial workmen – that was until lunchtime, when Taps took us for a walk in the village.

It was the hill that did it for me. The Celtic Poet noticed it too (fifteen years under his belt). Neither of us could remember the last time we had walked up a hill.

'Have you noticed how you have to lean slightly,' he said, 'and then adjust the angle of your ankles?'

'A bit like moonwalking,' I said.

It had never occurred to us before, of course, that we were missing hills in regulation prison exercise yards. We laughed about it, but we were fortunate that we had Taps in charge, giving us a bit of leeway to adjust. On the way back down the hill I told the Poet a story that Felix the Gambler had told me once, about an occasion when Felix was at a similar stage in his sentence after serving fourteen years – though his experience was not quite so quaint.

As part of the reintegration process in the jail Felix was in, Mrs Eccles, a large, jolly lady responsible for teaching 'life skills', would take a party of five or six men who were approaching the end of long sentences into the local town each month for 'acclimatization exercises' (crossing busy roads, working out bus timetables, making purchases etc.).

Apparently, these groups of mostly middle-aged men with their interesting hairstyles and clothes that were ten, twenty, or even thirty years out of date could be rather conspicuous. 'One geezer,' explained Felix, 'went out wearing purple flares and a yellow cheesecloth shirt – which wouldn't have been so bad, except that he was sixty-three and had long grey hair and an eye-patch.'

Determined to avoid being identified as an inmate from a long-term institution, Felix formed a plan. When it was his turn for a trip into town he borrowed a set of smart clothes from a wealthy associate, a man doing time for a 'white-collar' crime. When Mrs Eccles parked the prison minibus and began to shepherd the group along the pavement, Felix, in his pinstripes and crombie, discreetly dropped back several paces.

He bought a newspaper and pretended to read it when Mrs Eccles stopped at a busy intersection and proceeded to explain the complexities of the pelican crossing. Later, as Mrs Eccles and the group sat around a table in a coffee bar learning about 20p pieces and £2 coins, Felix stood at the counter talking racing form with the proprietor. 'I was having a great day,' he said, 'until... until...'

Until the supermarket incident. Even though years had passed and Felix had long since been recalled to prison, he still cringed at the memory. This is what happened. While the main group, baskets in hands, meandered around the supermarket behind Mrs Eccles, Felix adopted a sophisticated air and affected to study the wine display. It was then that he caught the eye of a pretty checkout girl. 'She smiled at me,' he said, 'so I smiled back, as you do.'

Several minutes of alluring glances and eyelash fluttering followed, and then, just as Felix, cool and suave, was preparing to saunter over and exchange a word or two with his budding paramour, he was stopped in his tracks by a holler. '*Feeelix!*' It was Mrs Eccles. She had a lesson to impart and all group members had to be present.

'I couldn't believe it,' said my embarrassed pal. 'She was three aisles away.' Not surprisingly the whole shop went quiet, as all eyes homed in on Felix. Mrs Eccles shouted again, 'Felix! Come and look at these offers. You'll need to know about special offers when you get released.' His cover blown, the red-faced gambler ducked his head and squirmed. The checkout girl watched disdainfully as he stepped quickly across the floor to join his sniggering peers.

'Can you imagine how he felt,' I said to the Poet at the bottom of the hill. 'Aye,' he said, 'it just goes tae show — we must never forget that this thing ain't over until it's over.'

7 March 2002

Catching up with the Celtic Poet

The Celtic Poet began his first unsupervised community work placement this week. This was good news in itself but the really good part is that the job is in a wildlife sanctuary five miles from the prison. For the Poet, a seasoned eco-warrior and believer in the rights of animals, it is a dream come true. We talked about it over the weekend. 'Phenomenal how things have worked out when you think about it,' he said. We were down by the old bike-repair shed and he was putting the finishing touches to the mountain bike he's been rebuilding over the winter. 'I know,' I said, eyeing the bike which would serve as his transport.

The Poet and I had spent around four years on the same wings and landings in the closed system before meeting up again in this jail. Although we were never close, there always seemed to be an affinity between us, an understanding of sorts. They were dour days, but he and I attended the same writers' group and it became clear that we held similar views on what prison should be about.

As a means of generating some optimism, at a time when hope was all we had, I did some research on low-security prisons with enabling regimes. 'If we ever get to go to open condi-

145

tions,' I said to him as I passed him a handful of bumph during the coffee break one evening, 'that's the place to aim for.' A couple of days later he was transferred.

I had no idea where the Poet ended up. The writers' group folded and soon he was no longer part of wing conversations. My reclassification order came through eventually and I was transferred north. I met a friend of the Poet's who told me he was in a B Cat in the east. 'But he's had a bit of grief – you know what he's like with his principles.' Diet was usually the problem. It had always been an issue between the Poet and prison kitchens. Though many prison cooks made stupendous efforts to accommodate dietary requirements, others didn't. And the Poet would rather starve than eat anything produced at the expense of an animal.

It had been more than three years, and funnily enough this jail was the very one that we had fantasized about during our last conversation. And there I was, washing my dinner plate, when I heard that familiar voice behind me. I'd only been here a couple of days. 'You made it, then?' How pleased I was when I turned around to find the long-haired, bearded one grinning broadly. 'Phenomenal,' he said, as we shook hands.

Inevitably, our first conversations consisted mostly of jail talk. We remembered B Wing in that old Midlands prison in the nineties. 'The Bronx,' he said. 'Beirut!' I responded. Cell fires, scalding, self-mutilation, ambushes, six suicides in two years. 'Just everyday tales of prison folk,' I said. So much had happened in the intervening years. 'You remember Biscuit?' he said. 'How could I forget him?' I replied, chuckling. Me and Biscuit – a superlative practitioner of mind-games – had had a few run-ins over the years, but managed to part on good terms when the time came.

'He's dead – cancer.'

'Christ,' I said.

'Remember Neady? Topped himself in Bedford prison.'

'Jesus,' I said. We all had demons to conquer, but Neady always seemed to have more than anybody else.

It didn't take long for us to tire of catching up. More recently our occasional talks have been about the future – a big step that is close now for my bike-riding friend. The other evening I was out walking with the Tank when the Poet came up in conversation. 'I know he is into the animal thing,' said the Tank (six foot four, twenty-one stone), 'but why do they call him the Poet?' I racked my brains and then remembered the first lines of a poem the Poet had composed as a wedding gift to his brother and new sister-in-law during one prolonged stint in a punishment block. He'd shared it with us one evening at our old writers' group and we had all been moved. I recited the lines to the Tank.

> *Watched a web-weaving spider*
> *spin out her yarn of sparkling hue*
> *between raindrops on my window*
> *as I wrote these lines for you.*
> *Ne'er fret about the blue or the borrowed,*
> *forget the old and the new,*
> *just thread your life together with spider silk*
> *and it will be strong and good and true.*

'Right,' said the Tank, 'I see.' And for the next twenty minutes we continued our walk in silence.

21 March 2002

The Kid's moment of truth

As I was listening to the Kid recount something that had happened to him on his way to his voluntary work placement I was struck suddenly by the magnitude of his achievement. Ten years in prison and still only twenty-six. Yet if you were to meet the Kid out there – on the street, in the shops – he would probably be the last person that you would ever suspect of being a serving prisoner on day release. Which was why I was initially wor-

147

ried for him when he explained the details of his encounter on the train. 'It was only a conversation,' he said, 'but it felt so meaningful, I didn't think I had any other choice.'

He had been sitting in an old-style carriage of individual compartments with seating for eight. For a while his seven fellow commuters did their best to avoid acknowledging each other's presence. Then he noticed that the elderly lady sitting opposite was reading a book with which he was familiar. The book, by a modern philosopher, had featured in the Kid's academic studies in prison and had assisted in his new understanding of society.

'She knows what she's talking about,' he said, when the lady eventually looked up. 'You've read her?' she asked, smiling. The discussion which followed encompassed globalization, domestic politics, and finally crime and punishment. By the nodding of heads and smiles of agreement it seemed that the other commuters were also enjoying the dialogue. It hadn't been planned, but the Kid admitted later that it had felt good to hold court with people who, if all went well at his next parole hearing, would soon be his fellow citizens. That was until the lady asked him, 'And what is it exactly that you do?'

The Kid's voluntary work involves working with disaffected young people in danger of being drawn into an 'offending lifestyle'. It is a cause to which he is deeply committed, which is why the young people with whom he works respect and listen to him. They know that he knows where they are coming from because, once upon a time, he was there too. But it was risky for the Kid to reveal his true status to strangers in a still largely unforgiving society. Perhaps he could say he was a youth worker. It was true after all – well, kind of. As he pondered the question his fellow passengers waited for the answer.

The main task for most people who end up inside is to try to emerge from the other end of the sentence mentally and physically intact. Young offenders and adult prisoners face similar challenges in many ways. Understanding the rules: that's a job and a half. Particularly when first of all you have to get your head around the idea that there are no rules. Of course there are official rules. But they bear no relation to the unwritten rules on the landings, none of which are hard and fast, and the recognition of which depends on so many variables – not least of which are the moods, demeanour, mental state and physical attributes of any prison wing's current inhabitants.

Young offender institutions (YOIs) are often little more than proving grounds for immature and maladjusted young men; gladiator schools rife with gangsterism, intimidation and fear. Which is why so many long-term YOs who have to transfer to adult prisons when they reach twenty-one are so ill-equipped for the transition. Few manage it well, certainly not as well as the Kid. Many drift from jail to jail in a state of stunted maturation, ending up stranded for ever somewhere between boyhood and manhood. They ingest so much jail culture that it almost becomes ingrained into their psyches. That is why the Kid's achievement is so huge. But it would be unfair to expect the average commuter to understand.

'So what did you tell the lady on the train with everybody listening?' I asked. 'I was going to lie,' he said, 'but then I thought about the journey I had made to get to where I am now and it just didn't seem right.' It was an unenviable dilemma he faced. In the end he told the truth. There was a nervous shuffle and a sharp intake of breath or two – naturally. But not from the lady. Instead she offered her hand and introduced herself with a warm, 'Very pleased to meet you.'

Wittingly or not, the lady did the Kid a great service with her gesture of acceptance and approval. On the other hand I would like to think that those present recognized that the Kid did them a service too. I'm not sure that he sees it that way himself, mind you, but one thing is for sure – we're going to have to stop calling him the Kid.

4 April 2002

Del has a crafty drink – but Mickey pays the price

You'll recall that when Mickey Folsom introduced me to his friend Del soon after I arrived in this prison, I was slightly uneasy when he appeared to overstate our past friendship. True, Mickey and I had both made a big deal of meeting up again. But our acquaintanceship merely stemmed from us having lived on the same wing of the same prison seven years earlier. At the time our association had barely stretched beyond the odd conversation in the meal queue. When we greeted each other here it may have looked as if we had once been close. But we were only pleased to see each other in the way that marathon runners who begin the course as strangers greet each other like comrades once past the finishing line. We had traversed the same demanding terrain and made it to a place of relative safety, that was all.

I was grateful to Mickey for his hospitality – showing me the ropes and inviting me to sit with him and Del in the dining hall – but I wasn't too sure about this new-found 'friendship'. There may be 'obligations' and I could do without those at this stage of my sentence. (You see how cynical and guarded jail can make a person?)

In fact I needn't have worried. With Mickey and Del out together working irregular shifts most of the time I hardly ever saw them except for weekends and occasional mealtimes. When we did meet up the conversation was always easy.

Del was funny, late middle-aged and totally incorrigible. His craggy face seemed to be constantly set in a smile – even though he was on his fourth prison sentence since Mickey started his twenty stretch twelve years ago. Mickey smiled a lot too, but there was also a serious side to him. It's one thing to be ducking and diving on the prison landings in your twenties or thirties. But at fifty, after a stint like the one he'd just done, it is a very different ball game – and he knew it.

'I'm never going to get another chance like this,' he said in the dining hall a few weeks ago. It was obvious he was committed. But I hadn't realized just how committed until Del told me that when Mickey's parole eligibility date had arrived shortly before I got here he had refused to make the application.

'He don't even want out early,' he said. 'Work, sleep, and save his money. That's all he wants to do.' Del sounded a little exasperated, which puzzled me for a while. It was only after several months that I came to understand the measure of their friendship.

Mickey and Del had been pals for a long time, since they were kids living on the same East End street. They had 'done a lot of bird' between them: sometimes together, sometimes not. From what I could gather, for years Mickey had been just as happy-go-lucky – until the twenty-year wake-up call. That was when Mickey got serious.

It made life a little awkward for him here though. He was dependent on Del for support during the last leg of his sentence. Del, however, had only been inside a couple of years this time, and with less than a year left to do he felt no real obligation to the open regime. That was why he was prepared to take a chance during his town visits. 'It's just a little tipple,' he'd say, 'for medicinal purposes.' Del thought it was funny, but not Mickey. 'You're gonna fack this up if you ain't careful Del,' he'd say. His friend would just grin and tell him to 'loosen up'.

Del had been here long enough to know what he was risking. The three absolutes in this place are: no violence, no drugs and no alcohol. Get caught indulging and there is no negotiation: you're on the next van to a closed jail. Perhaps if Del had served longer in the closed system he would have been more appreciative of a regime like this. Numerous twos, threes and fives might add up to a big lump over half a lifetime, but it will never compare with a straight ten, fifteen, or twenty in one go. Maybe, like Mickey, that's what he needed.

Del's number came up after his last town visit. It was a random breath test: every fifth man, and Del was number five. There were no tears, not from Del anyway. But Mickey did not take his pal's ship-out well at all. I saw him a couple of times last week in the dining hall. Sitting opposite his long face was hard work. I tried to talk to him, to pick him up. I owed him that. He didn't want to know. But when he failed to return from work on Friday night, I wished I'd tried harder.

18 April 2002

Five more years is a heavy price for one error of judgment

I received a good letter from Big Rinty this week. Upbeat as usual, though how he manages to maintain his sense of optimism when he's still wallowing in the same old mire beats me. 'Things are looking up,' he wrote. 'I've got a new brief.' I've heard that one before. By my reckoning that's at least his third in the last two years. Each time he gets a new lawyer, things begin to 'look up'. And all the while the time is ticking by.

The big news is that he's got a hearing next month. Rinty's life sentence is a 'discretionary', which means that he will appear in person in front of a panel comprising a judge, a probation officer and a psychiatrist to plead his case for release. It's make-or-break time for the big Dundonian. If he doesn't get a result it will be two years before he gets another hearing. By then he will be fifty years old and, I fear, no longer interested in freedom.

That's the danger, I suppose, of spending too long in a state of anticipation. Constantly focusing on reviews, waiting for 'answers' and having to pick yourself up after each knock-back, year after year after year. Rinty has been doing it since he began his sentence at the age of twenty-one. OK, so he had his chance. The DLP (discretionary lifer panel) he sat in front of in 1994 ordered his immediate release. The DLP was a brand-new mechanism then and the only issues they had to decide upon were: did the offender still present a danger to the public? And had enough time been served? Rinty got a 'no' and a 'yes', and the next morning found himself outside the prison gates.

It would be fair to say that he was unprepared for liberation. All he really had going for him when he walked out of that jail was his self-belief. But he was soon back on his feet. He found cheap digs and got a job with a charity as an administrator. Later he worked as a haulier, before leasing his own transport and becoming self-employed. Life outside turned out to be good for Rinty, for a while. Within a couple of years he had a flat, a car and a burgeoning business. If only his ambition had been sated.

Long-term prisoners often dream of one day achieving success in the outside world. When the odds are against you, as well as the world, and you're living the same old day over and over again, sometimes dreams are all that keep you going. When I first met Rinty in the mid-eighties he was the 'number one' in the charity transcription workshop where we both worked. It was a small place and the work we undertook required concentration, creativity and skill. The small workforce included a couple of former teachers, a former solicitor and a former company director, yet nobody could match the output of the Big Yin, whose only real qualifications prior to landing in prison had been surviving a basic education and a dysfunctional adolescence. 'This job has opened my eyes,' he told me once during a tea break. 'I could have had a career.'

And that was Rinty's dream – to have a career. Some chance, you would have thought, after a twenty-year stretch. Yet his chance came when he applied for the position of branch manager with a distribution company. It took balls, I'll give him that. In hindsight it would perhaps have been wiser to stick to haulage. Anyway, he bluffed his way through the interview and beat forty other candidates for the job (this was before life-sentenced prisoners released on licence were required by law to declare their convictions to prospective employers). Within months he'd been earmarked for promotion to area manager. Then came the dispute, an allegation, and a trial.

The jury was out for less than ten minutes and returned with a unanimous 'not guilty'. Under normal circumstances Rinty would have walked free, but the Home Office revoked his licence. 'They said I had to come back in for a psychological assessment,' he explained, after telling me the whole story. We were in my cell. That evening was the first time we'd seen each other in ten years. He was sitting on my bed. His short hair, swept back, was now grey and his skin sallow. 'For Christ's sake,' was the only response I could think of.

That was three years ago, which means he's now been back in for five. Rinty may have been foolish to get himself embroiled in a compromising situation out there. But jails are not geared up to turn out perfectly formed paragons of propriety. Five years, the equivalent of an eight-year sentence, was too heavy a price to have to pay for a momentary lack of judgment. Any more would be unnecessarily cruel. My fingers are crossed, Rint.

2 May 2002

The Experiment

The Experiment, the BBC's latest reality-TV offering, was flagged as 'a unique prison experiment'. But can it teach us anything that we did not already know? OK, so most people have now heard about the original prison experiment conducted by Dr Philip Zimbardo and two colleagues at Stanford, California in 1971. But for those who haven't, this is what happened.

Zimbardo constructed a makeshift jail in a closed basement corridor at Stanford University. Three cells were created by removing all the furniture from three classrooms and replacing the doors with steel-barred gates. A bed, mattress, sheet and pillow was all that was left in the cells, and a 2ft x 2ft x 7ft cupboard across the corridor served as a solitary confinement facility. The plan was to study 'prisoners and guards in a simulated prison'. The experiment was scheduled to last for two weeks.

Twenty-four 'normal, healthy male college students' were

recruited from the Stanford area as $15-a-day volunteer subjects. On a random basis, half were assigned to the role of guard and half to the role of prisoner. Three prisoners were allocated to each cell. The rest were on standby at their homes. The guards worked three-man eight-hour shifts and spent the rest of their time going about their usual lives away from the experiment.

Guards were issued with khaki uniforms, mirrored sunglasses, batons and whistles. Prisoners were given short muslin smocks, to be worn without underwear, rubber sandals and a cap each made from a nylon stocking. They were also required to wear a light lock and chain around one ankle to act as 'a constant reminder of the oppressiveness of the environment'.

Instructions were minimal. Guards were told only to do what they thought necessary to maintain 'a reasonable degree of order' (excluding physical punishment or physical aggression). Prisoners were given no guidance about behaviour 'appropriate for a prisoner role'. Clearly Zimbardo was seeking to maximize the spontaneity of his subjects' responses. But he sorely underestimated the volatile nature of the environment he had created.

After only two days some 'prisoners' began to show signs of distress, a response no doubt exacerbated by the over-enthusiastic behaviour of some of the guards. One of them, nicknamed John Wayne by the prisoners due to his swaggering, tough-guy manner, positively relished the power given to him by the role and made no apologies for 'contributing to the script' by systematically humiliating and bullying his charges.

Within a short time, five prisoner subjects had to be released due to 'extreme emotional depression, crying, rage and acute anxiety', and the experiment was prematurely terminated after six days; hence the controversy which followed.

What tends to be overlooked, however, whenever the Stanford University prison experiment is talked about, is that not all the guards became tyrants, and not all the prisoners broke down. Zimbardo said that he wanted to see what happened when he put 'good people in an evil place', and concluded that 'the evil place won over the good people'. Really? But prison buildings are neutral. Is it not that the people who live and work in them can be good or bad?

The fact is, Zimbardo's experiment showed that what happens when people are placed in a prison environment depends almost entirely on the motivation of those involved, their character types, and the quality of the interaction that takes place. Ethical considerations apart, this surely should have been the measure of the experiment's success. Instead, it became 'notorious' and 'infamous' for the way it graphically demonstrated the apparent corrupting influence of the power given to the guards and the resulting distress experienced by the prisoners when that power was abused. Well, well.

Even in the most developed society there is no doubting the necessity of imprisonment as a tool to help maintain social order. But the question is: does anybody really care about whether prisons have the potential to work to society's advantage? If the answer is 'yes' then have another look at the Stanford experiment. The message was stark and simple: it is people who make or break a prison. Zimbardo showed us all we needed to know. Further 'unique prison experiments' are superfluous pap.

16 May 2002

Unsupervised work outside the fence at last

These are the days that years ago I wondered if I would ever see. When I first arrived in open conditions it was difficult to accept the difference in people's attitudes. From the first warm welcome by the prison probation officer to the common courtesy of my fellow prisoners – holding doors open, respecting the order of meal queues, or just taking the time to assist when a new chap needed directions to some area of activity or other – it was all so alien. For weeks after I landed I found myself constantly thinking back to the dark places, the landings of the closed prisons, and asking nobody in particular, 'What the hell was that all about?'

Now it feels like the new beginning I always hoped it would be. For some months I have been going out in the prison van with the community work party, repairing public buildings, painting and decorating old folks' homes, youth clubs, scout huts and the like. Apart from the relatively short six-hour day (and the prison officer in civvies discreetly working alongside us while monitoring our conduct and assessing our risk potential), the experience is not so far removed from a normal working day in real life.

The community work party has two main functions, both equally important. Spare money is often so scarce in the community that many small repair and refurbishment projects might never get done if it wasn't for cheap prisoner labour. To this end, the initiative fosters good relations between the prison and the outside community. It also reintroduces prisoners to the reality of life outside.

Don't get me wrong. Breaking into a sweat is a phenomenon regularly experienced by people inside, though rarely as a result of a hard day's work. It's not because prisoners are any more averse to hard graft than people on the outside. But opportunities to do real work – the kind that makes your back ache and ensures a good night's sleep – are just so hard to come by in jail. Through the work party, prisoners on the verge of release can get used to the work routine again, which is probably the single most important factor in a successful resettlement programme. But then there is another, bigger step to be taken, and last week it was my turn.

The Celtic Poet was waiting when I returned to the house block. 'Well?' he said. It was hard to keep a straight face. The risk assessment board had sat to consider my case. I fitted all the criteria. No concerns had been raised. The presiding governor stamped the paperwork with 'Actioned'. 'I got it,' I said. 'I've been passed for unsupervised voluntary work in the community!'

The next morning after breakfast the Poet told me about the job he'd found me. 'Potholes,' he said. 'They need filling.' He could have told me that our task was to fill a disused quarry by hand and my smile would have been no less enthusiastic. The Poet took me through the procedures to get my licence (the piece of paper that would get me out of the gate unescorted). He introduced me to the activities officer and took me to meet the head gardener and pick up some tools. My voluntary work placement still had to be decided. In the meantime I was allowed to work on the roads outside the prison. 'That's it,' he said. 'Let's go.'

The Poet pushed the wheelbarrow and I carried the shovels. A female officer held the gate open for us. 'Mornin',' she said, adding, 'have a nice day.' Have a nice day? Was she kidding? The sun was shining, the birds were singing – it was all I could do to stop myself from bursting into a chorus of 'Heigh-ho, heigh-ho...'

We worked on the track by the copse at the back of the jail. Rolling green acres stretched out for miles. Nearby, rabbits played, occasionally startled by the sound of a woodpecker but seemingly oblivious to our manic shovelling and spreading. 'How does it feel then?' said the Poet when we stopped for a breather. At that moment a pair of Canada geese strolled by, shepherding a brood of young as they tumbled through the bluebells. It was one of the most beautiful sights I had ever seen. I never gave the Poet an answer. If I had I would have said, 'Undeserving.'

30 May 2002

It's goodbye to the Kid, who thrived – in spite of the system

The Kid looked anxious. It was nearly midnight and he was standing at my door with a sheaf of papers in one hand and half a cup of black coffee in the other. 'What's up?' I asked. 'Can I come in?' he said. I beckoned him inside and offered him my only chair. The parole board was due to consider the Kid's case for release the following week so I guessed that that was what he wanted to talk about.

It was to be an 'oral' hearing as opposed to a 'paper' one. As he had begun his sentence of Her Majesty's Pleasure when he was sixteen, the Kid was entitled to sit in front of a panel made up of a retired judge, a psychiatrist and a senior probation officer to argue his case. He could still submit 'reps' (written representations) to be considered along with the paperwork prepared by all the other report writers (and my advice to anyone I have ever spoken to in this situation has always been to do just that – never forgo any opportunity to give the decision-makers an insight into who you really are), but the Kid was already on the ball. The papers in his hand were his reps, and he was just calling to show me what he had written.

I had been here about a week when I first saw the Kid. I was having a haircut in the old kitchenette downstairs and he squeezed past me and the barber to get to the water boiler. 'Excuse me,' he said. Excuse me? He obviously hadn't been in jail very long, I thought at the time. His appearance, too, was unusual in the prison setting. Tall and blond, with a fresh, Scandinavian complexion. He looked nothing like your average con. It was a while later that we met properly, when I overheard him talking to an acquaintance about his 'tariff' (the portion of his sentence to be served in custody). Rudely, I butted in. Only lifers had tariffs: he couldn't be, surely. I had to ask him.

'HMP,' he said.

'Short tariff?' I asked.

'Ten years,' he said, adding, 'I've just had it reduced from twelve by the Lord Chief Justice.'

I had read about the LCJ's review of HMP tariffs following a European Court ruling. The Kid invited me to his room for coffee and explained further. I was impressed by his openness, but incredulous when he told me, 'I've actually done ten years now.'

He was obviously untainted by the system. He had educated himself, learned counselling skills and spent the previous four years in a medium-security prison working with the local youth-offending team, sharing his experiences with young people at risk who visited the jail as part of their rehabilitation orders. His role was to try to get them to understand where persistent offending could lead. The reduction in the Kid's tariff meant that parole reports had to be prepared immediately. All his outside activities had to be brought forward. Home leaves, town visits, community work. These were his 'tests', made more challenging by the fact that they had been thrust upon him without notice.

I read through his reps and smiled. Clear, concise, sincere. He had no need to be anxious. He was obviously going home. It was hard not to envy him. Here he was on the verge of a new life outside, at about the same age as I had been when I came in. But I couldn't fault him. In a way he epitomized what the system should really be all about. Except he had gained from the experience in spite of the system and not because of it. That was one of the reasons I admired him.

He was on a home leave when the board sat. He came back to the prison specially for the day. A week later he had his answer. The night before he left us, the Tank, the Poet and a couple of other unsavoury characters were sitting in his room, wishing him well and drinking his coffee. Suddenly the Kid spoke. 'You know what?' he said. 'Over the years I've sat in a few guys' cells the night before they were going home and now I can hardly believe that we're all sitting here and it's my turn.'

'Bless,' said the Tank. We all took it in turns to say our goodbyes. The Poet gave him some lines he had composed for the occasion. The next morning, before breakfast, he was gone. Ten years. Just like that. The end. Farewell to the Kid, good luck to the man.

13 June 2002

Cheerio Weevo

If he had planned to escape, why did he pick up the groceries? That was the question people were asking last week when Weevo went over the fence. Most thought it must have been a spontaneous act of desperation. The clue which led to that conclusion was that in the morning he had collected the orders from the prison shop for some of the lads who were out all day on paid work. And – to give him his due – he hadn't tampered with any of the stuff. When his room was searched that night, all the orders were still intact, still sealed in plastic bags. But therein lies another clue which, on the contrary, suggests that his decision to decamp was not made on the spur of the moment. Weevo liked drugs. That was why he was always broke. If his flight had been unplanned he would have needed money fast. There must have been £100 worth of phonecards in the orders he was holding. He would have had no problem cashing those in on the landings.

But it should never have ended this way. Weevo had been an asset to the jail. Like the majority of fixed-termers, he arrived as a C Category. To make D Cat, all he had to do was comply with the requirements of the regime – which he managed, in spite of his drug habit. He had a trusted job serving the tea and biscuits in the visits hall. He had completed his quota of days working with the supervised community work project. And, perhaps most endearing of all, by the end of the season he was the leading goalscorer for the prison football team. It took a little longer than usual for his D Cat status to be confirmed, mind you. For even though he had made his mark in the jail community, a drug problem in a place as open as this cannot be kept hidden for long.

It was his mood swings that gave him away: talking to everybody one day, talking to nobody the next. That and walking around blatantly 'pinned up' (pupils like pinheads – a sure sign that drugs are in the system). The authorities here had known before accepting Weevo that he had a drug history. But the deal was that this would be an opportunity to get clean. If he could take advantage of the regime, it would be a chance to make a fresh start when he got out. With only a year left to serve – not too long, not too short – he was ideally placed in his sentence.

But the advantage he was taking was the wrong one. He had been lucky with the mandatory drug tests. 'Smack' (heroin – Weevo's drug of choice) only stays in the system for three to seven days. A good flush with a gallon or so of water makes sure of that. And he was calculating with the voluntary drug tests. To show he was committed to changing, Weevo had volunteered for the 'frequent testing' programme – but then provided his sample from a small container of clean urine hidden under his crotch. 'Just another load of bollocks,' observed Weevo's pal, Crampon (who tells us that in another life he was a mountain climber).

So, with his problems unresolved, Weevo got his D Cat. Perhaps he would sort himself out once the pressure of waiting was off. At least that's what you wanted to believe, for his sake. Then, on his first unescorted town visit, he went to an unauthorized location and was spotted by an off-duty prison officer. Not only did he get 'grounded' indefinitely when he returned, but the governor also told him, 'We are considering making you a C Cat again – until you can prove that you're genuinely ready for your D Cat.'

That must have been too much for Weevo. Failing in an environment where every opportunity is provided to assist you in achieving success serves only to compound the failure. To be seen to be going backwards when everyone around you is apparently doing so well makes the situation even more difficult to accept – regardless of the fact that it's your own actions which have brought about the failure in the first place.

A week before he went, over a cup of tea in Crampon's room, he told his friend, 'They can shove their C Cat and they can shove their D Cat. In a little while I'm gonna be a free Cat!' Crampon kept this bit quiet until a couple of days after Weevo's 'breakout'. (The fence is high, yet as it's only a single-skinner and there's no razor wire it seems more suited to keeping the curious out than to keeping the prisoners in.) Along with the rest of the evidence, however, Crampon's revelation proves that Weevo's unorthodox departure was pre-planned. The picking-up of the groceries was obviously just a cover.

27 June 2002

World Cups or Wimbledons – we're all doing time

Time passing is not something people on the outside spend much time thinking about, I guess. Why should they? Not unless there's a specific reason: to reminisce about a relationship or a holiday, or perhaps to look forward to a happy event such as a birth or wedding. Otherwise everybody is just getting by and getting on as best they can in as painless a manner as possible.

On the other hand, no matter how focused you are in jail, there's no getting away from the constant looking back and looking forward – always trying to experience a palpable sense of time passing. Some people count the days. Others count the weeks or the months. My way was to note the national holidays. Easter was the first milestone in a new year; then May Day; the spring bank holiday; the August bank holiday – and then Christmas came and went and it was time to start again. I never counted the years, for the simple reason that so many had to pass before they had any real impact on the calculations.

The other day Agbo was talking about the time he had left to serve. We were sitting across from each other in the dining hall. I tried to impress him with a flash of profundity and said, 'Do you know, there are some philosophers who argue that there is no "past" and no "future"? They say that there is only "now".' I had read it somewhere, years ago. I couldn't remember where or when but it was always a good line to throw into these

163

conversations, to get people thinking and debating. Lifting his knife and fork from his plate, Agbo said, 'No disrespect mate, but I think that's a load of crap. When I was weighed off, it got to the summer and I thought to myself, three Wimbledons and I'll only have six months left. And that,' he said, referring to the most recent SW19 tournament, 'was number three.'

Three Wimbledons? I'd never thought of it like that before. Then Agbo said, almost apologetically, 'I know it's nothing compared to the bird that some of you long-term blokes have got to do, though.'

'But it's all relative,' I said, hoping he wouldn't ask how many Wimbledons I had done. It's not unusual for young fixed-term prisoners to become wary of some of the long-termers when they find out how long they've been in. The idea of someone living on prison landings for ten, fifteen or, like me, eighteen Wimbledons or more can be difficult for young men in their twenties to get their heads round. Along with Tel, who's doing a ten and sits next to me at mealtimes, and Rick, doing an eight, who sits opposite Tel, Agbo is a pleasant dining companion. I didn't want him to start thinking of me as some sort of oddball. At least not without getting to know me first.

'When you got your four years,' I continued, 'it must have felt like your world had come to an end.'

'It did,' he said. 'I thought the time was never going to pass. But it has, and now I'm looking back at three Wimbledons *and* a World Cup.'

Christ, I thought, don't mention World Cups. But the question had already formed in his mind. 'That's a point,' he said. 'If you don't mind me asking, how many World Cups have you been in jail for?' I looked down at my plate and then at Rick, who sniggered. Rick and I were both in another jail in the mid-nineties when he was on another sentence. He knew I was into double figures then.

'Well, let's see,' I said, working backwards in my head. 'There was this last one obviously, when Seaman was beaten with that unbelievable goal. Before that there was the Beckham kick at the

Argentinian, Simeone, for which Becks got the red card. Then it was the one when the Brazilians were the first to win the final on penalties. Before that it was the one where Gazza wept, and before that...' By this time Agbo was wide-eyed. 'Before that,' I continued, 'it was the one when the Hand of God scored a goal against England.'

'Maradona,' he said.

'That's right,' I replied.

'I was only nine,' he said.

'Mmm,' I mumbled.

'So all the time I was out there, growin' up, watchin' those games all those years, you was doin' time?' He looked shocked.

'Listen mate,' I said, 'don't worry about it. Wimbledons, World Cups, looking back, looking forward – inside or outside – we're all doing time.' Rick and Tel laughed at that while Agbo stayed quiet and carried on eating. I don't think he quite got it, though I'm confident he will eventually – when enough of his own years have passed.

11 July 2002

All mod cons

During a discussion about prisons, and in particular the purpose of imprisonment, a prison governor once said to me, 'Oh, we believe in rehabilitation, but we're not quite sure just how rehabilitated we want prisoners to be.' The conversation took place some years ago, but it was the first thing that came to mind when I read that the radical 'prisons of the future' plan, spelled out in a report published yesterday, had 'top-level backing'.

'You see,' said the governor during the same conversation, 'so long as society demands retribution from offenders, we have to be careful about allowing too much rehabilitation.' And there you have the weeping sore that has been festering at the heart of modern penal philosophy for the past hundred years or so. If there really has been a change in the attitudes of those in charge of running the prison system, and they are at last prepared to commit wholeheartedly to the idea that prisons should primarily be concerned with facilitating rehabilitation for prisoners, then there may indeed be hope for this new initiative.

The plans are impressive. The idea is that prisoners will live in individual house blocks located within a formidable perimeter wall. Each house will consist of a self-contained 'autonomous live-learn unit', designed to be secure, but humane to the highest possible degree. As education is to be the mainstay of the day-to-day regime, the houses are to be 'wired' for learning and working, with linked keyboards and screens in each cell allowing for study and communication via an intranet prison cable-television network.

The most sensible aspect of the new plan is the design of the cells. One of the main causes of psychological distress in a prisoner is enforced confinement in a small space. The new design may alleviate much of this effect by liberating the maximum amount of living space. For example, the bed, which in a regular cell takes up most of the space, is fixed high up on the back wall like the top tier of a bunk bed. Underneath the bed, in front of a large window, sit the table and chair – which leaves plenty of room for an easy chair. The en-suite WC and shower are in an ingeniously concealed compartment, allowing acceptable levels of dignity and modesty.

The cells are built in tiers over a number of floors, set in a U-shape around a central atrium. Lower floors incorporate venues for house meetings, leisure activities and dining. The ground floor on the south side opens on to a walled garden which can be used for 'sport, casual games, and as a kitchen garden to grow vegetables, fruit and herbs for the house'. The layout and structure of the building 'makes possible a different kind of social integration which more closely replicates conditions in the wider world'.

At least that is the idea. And it is an admirable one. The people who prepared the report apparently consulted groups of prisoners as the new plans were formulated, but the more I've looked at it the more I get the twinge of a feeling that these newfangled prison blocks have been designed with a view to holding model citizens only. An environment which is too clean, too ordered – in short, too 'posh' – may unwittingly present a threat to many of those who will have to live in it. I once saw how the transfer to a newly built wing that was bright, spacious and allegedly 'user friendly' had a disastrous effect on one man who considered himself more suited to the rougher fabric of the old-style wings. In protest he smashed the brand-new porcelain sink and toilet bowl on the first night, cutting himself badly in the process. Others were unhappy too but adapted eventually, though reluctantly.

Interestingly, the role of the prison officer in the new regime is to be transformed from mere gaoler to 'enabler', though it has to be said that there are a number of prison officers already in the system who see themselves as enablers. These men and women are prepared to make great efforts to assist development in their charges, and they shine on the landings like beacons. But nobody can blame the majority for their apparent disinclination towards change for the better.

For too long the prison system has accommodated a population that feels it has been used and abused by a succession of home secretaries, making the desperately needed fundamental change in attitudes on both sides almost impossible. A change in attitudes on the outside is even more important. Otherwise this scheme, commendable as it is, will be dismissed as a charter for 'holiday camps' and a waste of taxpayers' money.

Buildings may change, regimes may change, but unless there is a commensurate change in social attitudes we are going to be stuck in the same old rut for another hundred years or so.

18 July 2002

Temporary release gives just a taste of freedom

Question: when is a prisoner not a prisoner? Answer: when he is on temporary release. That is how it felt for a while, anyway. There is no denying that it was odd in the beginning. Especially that initial step. Being allowed to walk unescorted out of the prison gate after so long felt so normal, yet at the same time so strange. Would I be called back? ('OK, you didn't run. You've passed that test. Back you come.')

Would I be followed? Spied upon? Even though the senses feel locked on to the highest level of stimulation and fresh waves of euphoria are generated by the most banal scenes – people standing at a bus stop, a postman emptying a postbox – the feeling persists that it just cannot be right that I'm out here on my own. And odder still is the return. Walking back to the prison. Standing outside the gate. Pressing the bell to be let back in. The choice to stay or go, at last, is mine.

Long ago, I decided that this sentence was going to be as positive an experience as I could possibly make it. From that time on, I always saw my imprisonment as a means to an end. It took some time to work out exactly what that end was going to be. But one thing I knew from the start was that freedom, liberation, release – whichever term best describes the end of incarceration – was never my main objective.

Perhaps that is why this new stage of the sentence feels like it has arrived so quickly. Clearly I was prepared for it. The supervised work in the community obviously helped, as did the shopping trips to the local town with my case officer – 'escorted absences', as they are known officially. But looking back, the real preparation was the way I chose to do the sentence.

Having my own agenda meant that I had a measure of control over the way my life inside developed. I never yearned for the outside world, I never longed for experiences which were impossible to achieve in confinement. That in itself was a type of liberation. I was determined to live in prison and not merely 'do time'. Now the time has come to think about living on the outside. And this is the period of transition.

The options for undertaking unsupervised voluntary work are varied. Places are available in charity shops and local authority establishments, and as general helpers to less able members of society, such as the elderly or the sick. I considered all these and then remembered that I was once helped by an organization that runs an information centre for people with special needs. Its main office is just a train ride away. I knew it used volunteers, and applied. 'I've learned to type,' I wrote, 'I have good communication skills and I'm adept at lugging heavy things about.'

The reply from the administrator made me feel dizzy. 'We would be delighted to have you join us as a volunteer,' she wrote. 'We have a vacancy for an information officer.' I would have to keep the job title quiet among the lads, of course, but I accepted immediately.

I had already been out several times on my own to repair the dirt track outside the prison. But to go out in town clothes and join the throng of commuters – that was something else altogether. Walking the streets unaccompanied. Blending in with the crowds. Occasionally catching sight of my reflection in a shop window.

I was slightly nervous the first time I queued at the hatch at the train station. My turn came and I told the man behind the glass my destination. 'Return please,' I said. There was no question about whether or not I'd be coming back. Once on board I found a seat and settled down to enjoy the journey. The train seemed surprisingly old. It soon filled up, so much so that people had to stand in the aisles. Some read newspapers, some read books – and some had conversations on their mobile phones. 'Hi, I'm on the train…' Like a visitor from a foreign land I observed and mentally noted it all.

Now I am a regular commuter. Three days a week I work in an office. The people with whom I work are warm and accepting and treat me like a colleague. There are so many reasons why it would be easy to forget my status. But real freedom beckons – a far greater reason not to forget. In the meantime I'll enjoy this experience for what it is, and remember that temporary release is just an extension of the boundaries.

25 July 2002

My recurring nightmare and Big Rinty's reality

For some time before receiving the news that I had been downgraded to Category D and suitable for open conditions, I'd been troubled by a recurring dream. In the dream I wake up in a prison cell, locked, bolted and heavily barred. (Considering how many years this has been a reality you might think that it was not much of a dream.) I take in the scene through one half-open eye and then confusion turns to panic. After a period of freedom following my release something has happened. I've been 'recalled'. I'm back inside. I jump out of bed and start hammering on the door with my fist and shouting, '*There's been a mistake! There's been a mistake!*' And then I wake up for real. Oh sweet relief. Almost tearful joy. Everything's fine. I'm still in jail.

The dream occurred again last week – the first time since my transfer to this low-security prison. The only difference this time was that it lasted much longer than usual, which exacerbated its effect. As I lay in the dark after waking, damp with sweat and heart still pounding, I thought about why it should start again. Probably two reasons, I decided. First, now that I am going out into the community to do voluntary work, I am often confronted with precious freedom. Perhaps the wonder I feel in all I see out there is creating a subconscious fear of having it taken away again. Second, and the clincher I think, was the latest letter I received from my pal Big Rinty. The big Dundonian served almost twenty years of his life sentence before being released, only to be recalled to prison five years ago after three years of freedom, and his situation concerns me greatly.

He didn't look too bad the first time I saw him after a ten-year interlude. When he stuck his head around my cell door soon after I had landed in the medium-security jail, I recognized him immediately. The short grey hair and pale skin were new features, but they did nothing to dim that Rinty smile. It was good to see him again, though I hesitated to tell him that in the circumstances. I was just so amazed that he was coping with his situation so well.

After he'd finished recounting the story of what had happened to him, I said, 'So a complaint was made. You went on trial. The jury took eight minutes to find you not guilty. And then you were recalled to prison?'

'Correct,' he said.

'And how long have you been back in?'

'Two years,' he said.

Two years is the equivalent of a four-year fixed sentence (only half of any sentence of four years or under is served in custody). When I asked him what his prospects were for getting back out again he said, 'You tell me.'

I could have understood if the jury had found him guilty of an offence. And after spending a long time thinking about it I could even understand the Big Yin getting recalled for a not guilty, maybe for a period of assessment so the authorities could ascertain if there were any serious problems that needed addressing. But to just lock him up and leave him to adapt to long-term imprisonment again after he proved he could function competently outside seemed totally unfair to me.

Eventually Rinty was persuaded to do offending-behaviour courses. One lasted six weeks, and one lasted almost a year. The tutors on both courses gave him glowing reports and recommended that he should be returned to an open prison at the earliest opportunity, but the treatment manager overruled them. 'Remain in closed conditions,' he said. 'More courses.' (Remember, up until 1994 when Rinty was first released there was no such thing in prison as an offending-behaviour course.

The system Rinty returned to was vastly different to the one he left.)

But Rinty made a stand. 'I'm going to fight this,' he told me long before I moved. It would all depend on his next hearing, in front of a panel comprising a judge, a probation officer and a psychiatrist. The panel would have the final say. They sat in June, almost five years to the day that he was recalled – the equivalent of an eight-year sentence.

There was no letter in June, so I guessed it was going to be bad news. When there was nothing in July I knew. 'Well,' he wrote in last week's, 'the worst-case scenario arrived with a bang...' And what a bang: transfer to another closed prison, undertake another offending-behaviour course, further review in no later than two years' time.

It's worse than my dream – a genuine nightmare in fact, except there's no waking up, and Rinty is living it.

8 August 2002

Who is going to employ a man with a criminal record?

Sooner or later, I have to attempt to join the ranks of people on the outside who work for a living. The date when I am allowed – no, expected – to take paid work is looming. You would think that after waiting so long to reach this stage of the sentence I'd be happy about it, or a little excited at least. Instead I am feeling agitated and, for the moment, just a little nervous. But it has to be faced eventually. 'So why not sooner rather than later?' I thought last week when I spotted an advert for a job in a local paper that I believed would suit me down to the ground.

How different I felt when, shortly after arriving here, the activities governor first talked about the prospect of me entering the job market again. 'That's why we are called a "resettlement prison",' he said. 'If we can get a man into paid work before he is discharged, then it creates a more realistic possibility that he will return to society less inclined to reoffend. Stands to reason, doesn't it?'

Well, it did to me. It was one of the best bits of news I'd ever heard. He explained the different levels of the regime that I would be expected to achieve during my time here as I underwent the resettlement process. 'You have dates,' he said, 'and so long as you are meeting your targets, those dates are set in concrete.' This was so different to usual prison life. Nothing in the closed system was ever 'set in concrete'. On the contrary, 'targets' could be missed by months, and sometimes even years.

The governor told me that, eight weeks from when I landed, I would have a 'reception board'. So long as there were no hiccups (a positive drugs or alcohol test, or a violent incident, for example), the board would pass me for supervised voluntary work in the community – and that's just what happened. He said that four months after that (during which time I would be constantly monitored), and following a detailed risk assessment, I would be passed for unsupervised voluntary work in the community. 'Again,' he said, 'so long as no problems arise.' I knew what kind of problems he was talking about. I'd met enough fellow prisoners in the system who had been sent back to closed prisons for 'breach of trust', or 'breach of licence conditions'. I hoped I wasn't being complacent, but short of a stitch-up, I couldn't see a situation arising in which I would be careless enough to get involved in anything which would jeopardize my position.

Sure enough, six months later to the day (just as the governor had predicted), I was walking out of the gate on my own to work three days a week for a charity organization. 'And then, of course,' the governor said, reaching the end of that discourse on resettlement, 'after six months of successful voluntary work, you'll be able to take paid employment.' This was the bit that really took my breath away. I knew that people here worked outside. Associates from days gone by who had arrived long before me were working outside as drivers, factory hands, industrial cleaners. 'I can't wait for that,' I told the governor, truthfully.

And the truth is that I'm still as enthusiastic as ever about getting a job and a wage – a real wage. (The top wage for a thirty-hour week in prison when I came in eighteen years ago was £2.75; now the most I can earn in prison as a cleaner is £8.50 a week.) But when I spotted the advert in the paper, the reality of my situation suddenly hit me.

I was confident that as far as the job description was concerned I would be an ideal candidate, so I sent off for an application form anyway. Whether or not the employer would understand that it was my time in jail that had enabled me to become someone fit to hold a responsible job, I couldn't say.

But let's suppose I get as far as the interview stage. I turn up at the company. I am shown to an office. I knock on the door and enter. Three people in suits, or maybe five, are sitting behind a long table; facing them across the table, one chair: empty.

'Come in. Please, sit down,' says the one in the middle.

'Thank you,' I reply.

The spokesperson continues, 'We see you ticked the box affirming that you have a criminal record.'

'Yes,' I say.

'Can you tell us about that, please?'

'Well, erm, it all started when I was ten...' I say, lowering my head. In the imagined version that's as far as I get.

22 August 2002

Some people on the outside are living in their own prisons

It's easy to forget when you're in jail that people on the outside have problems too. I've lost count over the years of the number of times that prison officers have told me, 'It's hard out there, you know.' My silent mental response was always, 'Is that right? You want to try doing a few years in here then.' But all problems are relative I suppose.

The smartly dressed man I found myself sitting next to on the train one evening had problems. I was returning to the prison after another day's unsupervised voluntary work. As usual the train had been full when it arrived at my station. My journey takes about forty minutes and normally I spend it standing in a doorwell looking out of the open window and admiring the views between stops.

But that evening, as the train pulled to a halt, I spotted the one empty seat in the carriage, which for a change stopped with a door directly in front of where I was standing. Pleased with my slice of good luck, I hopped on and plonked myself down next to Mr Pinstripes, who was sitting by a window.

After a couple of embarrassing incidents I had learned not to acknowledge people on the train when entering. It still seems odd, though, to sit so close to fellow travellers, all of us ignoring each other — especially after years of the forced familiarity which exists on prison wings. Blanking someone in prison as you pass them on a landing can have dire consequences. It makes no difference if you have never set eyes on the person before in your life. A polite nod and an 'All right mate?' reciprocated during such an encounter ensures that no offence will be taken and stewed upon by either party. It often means that you end up greeting the same people a dozen times or more a day. But getting blanked, even by a stranger, is tantamount to receiving a threat and an outright challenge in a high-security jail. Better to be safe than sorry.

So I've discovered that commuters are not particularly friendly, but neither do they appear to go out of their way to be unfriendly. At least I hadn't met a hostile one until I encountered Mr Pinstripes. We were only five minutes out of the station when his mobile phone began to ring. He fumbled for it in his jacket, then flicked it open and spoke. 'I'm on the train,' he said. A woman with crimped hair sitting opposite him reading a book glanced up at him and then looked at me. I thought that she and

I were going to exchange a knowing smile, but no. Before I could raise my eyebrows to indicate a shared disapproval, she'd blanked me.

'The marriage vows meant nothing to you,' said Mr Pinstripes into his mobile. The woman kept her head down. I tried to read my newspaper. Whatever response Mr Pinstripes got – he could only have been talking to his wife – he hadn't been placated. 'You proved it,' he retorted angrily.

I know it was none of my business. And I've got used to switching off my conversation receptors in the presence of people talking into mobile phones in public. But I'd heard what I'd heard and I knew that, apart from the young man facing me with eyes shut and Walkman earphones blaring, the rest of the people in the carriage must have heard it too. It was impossible to ignore this one.

'Whatever happens, you're not getting the house,' he continued, reaching down between his legs and retrieving a can of strong beer. 'No fucking way,' he said, and then he took a long pull at the alcohol.

By this time he was making me nervous. Unable to read because of the mounting tension, I'd been merely staring at my newspaper with my elbows on the armrests on either side of my seat. Suddenly Mr Pinstripes swore again into his phone, flicked it shut and shoved it roughly back into his pocket. He took another swig of his beer and rammed his elbow against mine, knocking my arm off the rest.

Retaliation would have been pointless. He was obviously in emotional pain and not thinking rationally. If anything, he needed somebody to talk to, and if his mind had not been so clouded with drink I might even have volunteered. I didn't feel that I'd lost anything by ignoring his assault. For, like him, I was just another stranger on a train.

We arrived at my stop and it was a relief to leave my belligerent travelling companion behind. Twenty minutes later I was pressing the gatehouse bell. It's not a good feeling going back to jail after a day spent in the free world. But that night it could have been worse: I could have been in Mr Pinstripes' shoes – going back to his prison.

5 September 2002

Good news for Tam – at last

Getting a job was never going to be easy. I knew that. But I wrote off for that application form nearly a month ago now and I expected a response at least, even if it was only the impolite version of 'go away'. I never thought for a moment that I was actually in with a chance of getting the job, and I was sceptical about whether I'd even get an interview. But it hadn't occurred to me that my prospective employer might ignore my politely written missive altogether.

Yes, I gave the prison address. But I didn't say how long I'd been inside. I didn't want to scare them off too soon. I'd learned that lesson after speaking to Tam the Man, a jolly, barrel-shaped neighbour also doing life, whose job-hunting adventures in the outside world are legendary in here. One small step at a time, I decided. That was the only way if there was to be any hope of me ever meeting a potential boss face to face.

In the meantime, the good news this week is that Tam has managed to get a job at last – after 104 applications and forty-three interviews. And, coincidentally, his very first application had elicited pretty much the same kind of response that I've just encountered, the only difference being that his enquiry had been made via the telephone.

'Hello?' said a pleasant voice on the other end of the line when Tam called.

'Hello,' said Tam. 'I'm ringing about the job.'

'Just a minute while I put you through,' said the sweet voice.

'Hello?' said a more formal male voice moments later.

'Hello,' said Tam again. 'About the job…'

'OK, I'll just take some details.'

'I have to tell you first though,' said Tam, 'I'm still a serving prisoner. But I'm allowed to work outside. It's a resettlement prison...'

'That's not a problem,' said the formal voice. 'May I ask the date of your conviction?'

Tam has a fistful of qualifications relating to the work he was applying for, including City and Guilds certificates and NVQs. He has a good discipline record and good institutional work reports. He was hoping to tell the person he was speaking to why he thought he would make a good employee before the issue of his imprisonment was discussed in any depth. But the question was asked too soon and Tam was obliged to answer.

'Erm... 1979.'

After a pause, the formal voice said, 'Was that another sentence?'

'No,' said Tam, 'it's the same one.'

There was another pause, longer this time.

'Hello?' said Tam. Then again, 'Hello? Hello?'

Then he heard the gentle click of a handset being replaced. But it didn't put him off. He's had so many knock-backs during his epic prison sentence that the rebuff hardly registered on his personal scale of disappointments. And there were more to come.

'If you're lucky enough to get an interview,' he told me once, 'don't get your hopes up. I've been to so many and as soon as I tell them my sentence – as we have to by law – and how long I've been in, you can see it in their faces, "How can we get rid of this bloke without offending him?"'

Tam's resilience was inspiring. And though there is a certain exterior brusqueness to his personality, you don't have to spend a long time talking to him to discover the warm and affable character that's being shielded. Then you start to like him and begin to wonder why he has been in prison for so long.

A few months ago Tam's close friend the Celtic Poet told me that Tam was released once. It took him a while to get on his feet, but he was getting by, until the day he bought a couple of pairs of jeans 'cheap from a man in a pub'. The magistrate was not impressed. 'For receiving stolen goods,' the pillar of society told Tam, 'four months in prison.'

'When was that then?' I asked the Poet. 'Over nine years ago,' he said.

Tam's involvement with the stolen jeans led to the Home Office revoking his life licence and having him recalled. It had taken him nine years just to get back to open conditions.

Knowing Tam's story made me wonder how he had any energy left for job-hunting. But I've never seen him down or heard him complain. And now he has proved that persistence is everything.

On reflection, my experience was a little disappointing. But imagine if I'd got an interview or, worse still, actually got the job. How on earth would I have been able to face Tam?

19 September 2002

Brace yourself, Jeffrey

Jeffrey Archer's ship-out from his open prison back to closed conditions last week caused me to flinch empathetically when I learned of his new location – Lincoln prison. For Lincoln features in my own prison career, although not in any significant way. In fact, the best thing I remember about my stay in that less than salubrious establishment some years ago is that it was mercifully brief. Just two days and nights in fact (a 'lodging') during a transfer from one long-term prison to another.

Lincoln is a classic Victorian prison with wings four tiers high fanning out from a cavernous centre. The idea behind the design was that warders could see and observe prisoners on every landing of every wing from the centre, thus ensuring that order, penitence and cleanliness (the primary concerns of the prison system in those days) were assiduously maintained.

By the time I got there in the mid-nineties, however, such

admirable expectations had long since been abandoned. My first thought as the big gates opened and swallowed up the van carrying me and half a dozen other men was that we were being taken back in time. Not, it has to be said, back to the Victorian golden age but, for me, to the time ten years earlier when my sentence had begun. For most long-term prisoners start off in prisons like Lincoln, Wandsworth, Winchester, Armley and the Scrubs. These are all 'local' prisons, whose population consists mainly of unconvicted prisoners held on remand while awaiting trial, and recently convicted prisoners awaiting allocation to prisons of varying categories (depending on the seriousness of their offence and the length of time they have to serve).

Perhaps that is why there is so much apathy in such places. Nobody is ever there for very long and those who are there spend most of their time banged up behind their doors, defenceless against the tide of enforced idleness. Overcrowding makes access to showers and clean clothes limited, which explains the gamut of human smells that combine and hang in the air with a lingering constancy, permeating the fabric of the building and curdling the atmosphere.

The processing routine that first night in Lincoln was pure cliché and perfectly reminiscent of my first night in my first local all those years earlier. Nothing had changed. The reception area was chaotic. Orderlies rushed backwards and forwards with items of kit, and a scattering of prison clothes lay across the cold, tiled floor. Several prison officers stood behind a long, white-topped counter. Our handcuffs were removed and, one by one, we were called to the counter. I stepped up first. In full view of more than a dozen people, one of the prison officers said curtly, 'Right, young man. Strip off and put your clothes in this box.' I did as I was told and eventually stood wearing only my underpants. 'Don't be shy,' said the officer, smirking at his colleagues. 'Let's have your Jockeys.' Not a nice memory. Especially since it had taken years to develop the persona which kept me safe on the long-term landings. But I took a deep breath and complied. My reward was an ill-fitting prison outfit and a coarse bedroll. You become hardened to the minor indignities of prison life by keeping in mind that, though it may feel as though the opposite is true, none of it is personal.

By pure numerical chance, I ended up that night in a cell on my own. To reach it, I walked through a grubby-looking wing, past a group of men sitting in hard-backed chairs, their heads tilted up towards the television high on a shelf in a corner. The bright colours of the holiday programme *Wish You Were Here...?* flickered incongruously in the gloom. In spite of the half-light, I couldn't help noticing the flaking paint on the walls, the bent and rocking railings along the gantries, and the sagging safety netting stretched between the upper floors. It seemed as if ingrained grime was evident in every corner, nook and cranny. My memory may be playing tricks on me but I would wager a week's prison wages that I saw cockroaches the size of small mice scuttling in the shadows. There was no toilet in the cell, just a battered looking plastic bucket, the inside of which was covered with a thick crust. No running water, a torn and stinking mattress, graffiti, detritus under the bed, a broken wooden table, no chair... Enough.

The fact is that, in practical terms, local jails are little more than depots: warehouses which hold and process an endless stream of human traffic, year in, year out. They are the leviathans of the prison service; too old and out of date to serve any genuinely positive purpose, but too big and useful – and necessary in fact, given the pressure the service is under – to get rid of.

Due to the perception that Archer was having too much of an easy time during his sentence in 'soft' North Sea Camp, it has been reported that Lincoln prison is a 'hard' jail, full of 'robbers, murderers, muggers and other assorted tough nuts'. In one sense, this stereotypical generalization is true – although the same could be said of almost any prison in the country, including open prisons.

The description of it being 'hard' inside a prison like Lincoln is a little misleading, however. They are scary places – there is no doubt about that – especially when first entering. But once a new prisoner has acclimatized to the environment, in an odd sort of way these local prisons can turn out to be quite cosy places. If you disregard the high suicide figures and incidences of self-harm – and Lincoln's are among the highest in the country – the fact is that those who adapt quickly do relatively easy time. Plus, it used to be the case that the majority of staff at these places had worked there for an eternity and would often treat prisoners more like naughty nephews than hardened criminals. Think Fletcher and pals and their capers with Mr Mackay and Mr Barrowclough in *Porridge* and you have as close a depiction of life in a traditional local jail as you are ever likely to get.

Nevertheless, my brief stint at Lincoln was a shock, probably because by then I was a seasoned campaigner, a veteran of the long-term system where I had learned how to survive on the landings and serve time constructively. Long-term prisons may be destructive and hostile places and can rightly be described as jails where 'hard time' is served. But they also have regimes which can be utilized and taken advantage of to enable personal development and advancement. The relationship between staff and prisoners in long-term prisons is generally less parental, so genuine respect between people on both sides of the fence is often able to flourish.

I would like to think that since my fleeting visit to Lincoln conditions for those within its confines have improved. But, though steps to eradicate the more unedifying aspects of the regime have undoubtedly been made, reports down the years leave me doubting that things have changed all that much.

The good news for Archer, however, is that he won't be there for very long. But maybe he will be there just long enough to reflect on this: it takes some prisoners a long, long time to get to an open prison. Some will never achieve it. To reach a stage in a prison sentence when you can meet a friend outside on a sunny day, or share a meal at home with a loved one, or even get the chance to actually drive your own car again – to gain these privileges from inside prison – is a precious achievement indeed.

30 September 2002

Driving lessons: a taste of being in control at last

It's not often that you get a chance to be in the driving seat in prison. Decisions are made for you. Permission has to be requested constantly. Control is in the hands of the man with the key. Empowerment may be achieved using guile and manipulation – or revolt even. But as far as the rest of the outside community is concerned, being a long-term prisoner is like being a long-term passenger. Which is probably why it came as such a shock recently to find myself literally in the driving seat – when I began taking driving lessons.

I had planned to take lessons eventually, if I ever got released properly. But I was prompted to apply for them in here after finding out a few months ago that it was possible, from the man who lives in the room opposite. 'You need to see the lady in education who coordinates work-related training courses,' he said. 'You can get a grant.'

In fact, it wasn't that simple. My interview with the lady in question, Mrs B, took place soon afterwards. First, I had to tell her why I needed to be able to drive. My answer needed careful consideration. I had it in mind to explain that I thought of a driving licence as a document of legitimization: a symbol of responsible citizenship. For as long as I can remember, my main ambition in life has been to one day become a regular member of society. Owning a full driving licence upon release would help to authenticate my membership, I believed; it was another ticket of entry. But before I could reveal these noble sentiments, she said, 'To get assistance from the prison's vocational fund, there has to be a practical reason. It has to be work-related.'

Of course. How naive of me. 'Well, I've been in prison a long time,' I said. 'A driving licence will enhance my chances of finding work.' That was enough to get me an interview with one of the vocational fund administrators, who approved my application 'on condition you contribute a third of the cost of the lessons'. Several begging letters to addresses supplied by Mrs B and a favour from a friend later, I had enough money to apply for a provisional licence, book the instructor and commence.

Even though I was well into my second decade in jail, it hadn't been long since I'd travelled by car. Several times over the years I had been transferred from prison to prison in taxis. Granted, I was always in the back, handcuffed between a couple of large prison officers. But at least I had been able to observe the process of driving fairly close up. It didn't look too compli-cated, I recalled. And anyway, driving a car is like riding a bike, isn't it? Once learned never forgotten? I soon discovered that this was only partly true.

'You've driven before?' asked the instructor, after introducing himself as Harvey and signing my attendance book.

'Er, yes,' I said, 'but it was some time ago.'

'How long have you been inside then?' he said.

It was a perfectly natural question under the circumstances, but almost the worst one he could have asked. My mind froze, and I felt trapped behind the wheel of the little Japanese car. Supposing I told him the truth. I could just imagine the ensuing silence, the embarrassed unease, and us confined so close together for the next two hours. So, reluctantly, I decided to fib.

'Er, four years,' I said, plucking a figure out of the air.

'Bloody hell,' he said. 'Have you got long left?'

Early on in my career as a menace to society, at the age of about sixteen, I had taught myself to drive after buying an old Ford Anglia for £30 from 'one careful lady owner'. I didn't take a test, and by my early twenties I must have broken most of the road-traffic laws. This opportunity was so important to me – but Harvey's questions were displacing my enthusiasm, my optimism and my confidence.

'Not long now,' I said. Relatively speaking, this wasn't a total untruth and Harvey seemed satisfied.

'Right, let's go,' he said. 'Let me have a look at what you can do.'

Two hours later we were back. Me sweating; Harvey red-faced. The driving lesson had been like a rollercoaster ride – with me in charge of the controls! Harvey's bald head seemed to be glowing. He took off his glasses and rubbed his eyes. 'Well, there's hope,' he said at last. 'There's definitely hope.'

I grinned and nodded. 'There's always hope, Harvey.'

Further progress to be reported.

3 October 2002

Stale porridge

The first instalments of Jeffrey Archer's autobiographical prison diaries, serialized this week in the *Daily Mail*, have revealed what most reasonable people who have not yet experienced it must have always suspected: that life in the British prison system does, in fact, have its downside. Archer's description of his first days in HMP Belmarsh – arguably the most secure prison in the country – certainly contrasts with reports that he was enjoying the 'good life' in North Sea Camp open prison up until two weeks ago.

The disgraced peer, who is currently in Lincoln prison where he was transferred for allegedly breaching the terms of a day-release licence while at the open jail, begins his blow-by-blow account from the moment his trial judge, Mr Justice Potts (supposedly 'unable to hide his delight'), hands down his four-year sentence. So begins what the *Mail* describes as his introduction to 'a world of humiliation and degradation'. As far as I can tell from reading the extracts, however, the worst thing that happens to him on his first day is that he is handcuffed to a female prison officer he rather ungallantly describes as 'overweight, around five foot three and has a cigarette dangling from her mouth'. The woman in question then walks him on to the prisoner transport wagon where he is installed in a cubicle for the short trip from the Old Bailey courthouse to the notorious Belmarsh.

Archer hints that the jury may have got it wrong when it

found him guilty and his co-accused, Ted Francis, not guilty of the same charge (asking, somewhat aptly in a soliloquy, how the two of them could have conspired to pervert the course of justice if one of them 'didn't realize that a conspiracy was taking place' – ah the mystery of the conspiracy laws). But to be fair to him, he appears determined not to convey any sense that he might be wallowing in self-pity in the telling of his story.

Neither can he be accused of glamorizing prison life. If anything, he understates how sensational this new experience must have been for a world-famous author used to a lifetime of success and high office – to the point that it is almost quite a plodding read, though mine may be a biased view simply because I know the world he is talking about so well. To me, being asked to 'strip' before being allocated a 'stark, cold and unwelcoming cell' measuring just 'five paces by three' and with 'thick iron bars' on the windows and poor sanitary facilities was old hat a long time ago.

Nevertheless, it takes a formidable constitution to get through a stint at a jail like Belmarsh and emerge unscathed at the end of it. The south London prison had not yet been built when I began my sentence. All I know of the place comes from what I have heard on the grapevine, mostly hearsay and rumour, but that has always been enough to make me thankful that I have never had to spend any time there. Prisoners who start off at Belmarsh usually get automatic respect when they arrive at other prisons – which demonstrates the fearsome reputation it has created for itself in the eleven years since it opened.

In the hard prison stakes, Belmarsh is the new Parkhurst. So for a man unused to violence and aggressive confrontation and more accustomed to the finer things in life (used to clothes, he pointedly informs the reader, designed by 'Aquascutum, Hilditch & Key, and YSL', and to dining at Le Caprice) I think Archer deserves credit for surviving his relatively brief time there so well.

On the other hand, he deserves no credit for writing about some of his fellow prisoners in a way in which they could be identified. Not only is this against prison rules but, for the highest-profile prisoners he names, it is grossly unfair and amounts to the abuse of powerless men already enduring wretched lives.

Why he felt he had to do this is unclear. It may well be that some prisoners were seduced into signing away their right to anonymity. But securing such valuable agreements with people when they are in the precarious state of incarceration – no matter how eager and competent they may appear on the surface – was a questionable deed at the very least.

We learn very little from Archer's dehumanizing commentary about the men he meets, other than the reasons for their imprisonment. And, bizarrely, everyone he does meet seems eager to share their secrets with him or – not so surprisingly – to helpfully reveal the secrets of others. A young Pakistani man tells him how he beat up his wife when he 'found her in bed with another man'. A lifer explains that the press misreported his crime and that he never shot his lover's boyfriend as reported but 'stabbed him seventeen times'. The same lifer points to a man in the exercise yard who never talks and explains, 'He killed his wife and young daughter.' (Around every corner Archer seems to find 'murderers' lurking. They're 'playing cards' or 'watching television'. One even offers to 'bump off' one of the prosecution witnesses at his trial, he reports malevolently.)

This is a lazy, intrusive way to write about prison life and serves little purpose other than to titillate and entertain at the expense of the vulnerable. Archer of all people should know that the reason a person is in prison – no matter what the crime – is but one small element of who that person is.

It is reported that 'Lord Jeff' (as he claims to have been addressed by his fellow prisoners) apparently has no regrets about having possibly broken prison rules again if it means he is able to highlight 'serious problems in the overcrowded jail system'. On this point I would have been in accord had his views been constructive. The prison system is an over-large and unwieldy organization, growing unnecessarily by the day. But it is too easy merely to complain about 'conditions'. As for the need to highlight the problems in our jails, weekly media stories of prison overcrowding, occasional disturbances, and critical reports issued regularly by HM Inspector of Prisons have been doing just that for as long as I can remember. So why should he think that society will take more notice of 'revelations' by someone as discredited in the eyes of the public as he is?

Jeffrey Archer is a successful novelist. When he was sent to prison an opportunity to write the book of his life and really make a difference presented itself. On the evidence of the diary extracts published so far, however, it is clear that he has missed that opportunity. One final note. Archer tells of the seventeen-year-old accused of shoplifting who lives 'surrounded by murderers, rapists, burglars and drug addicts', and asks, 'are these the best tutors he can learn from?' It is a fair observation – but it would have smacked more of sincerity if among his rogues gallery he had not forgotten to include 'perjurers'.

9 October 2002

A year since Cody was let out on bail

It's hard to believe that a year has passed already since Cody was released on bail. Our friend Cody. Warm, entertaining, resilient – and respected by all those who knew him on every prison wing he lived on for the twenty-four years he was inside, despite not a day passing during his imprisonment when he did not protest his innocence to the authorities. Yet even though he has been allowed to go home pending a fresh appeal hearing against his life sentence, Cody's difficulties are not over.

I knew Cody for only a relatively short time before he was bailed – a couple of years or so. We met for the first time when I was buffing the floor on my spur one day, over the teatime bang-up. The regular landing cleaner was in the seg unit hiding from drug debts and so several of us had volunteered to take it in turns to do the floor until another cleaner could be found.

There was no payment for the job, just the treat of being out and about when everybody else was locked behind their doors. While the landing officer had his feet up in the office, you could buff away and daydream to your heart's content, the drone of the buffer's motor enhancing the therapeutic effect.

I'd been buffing for about twenty minutes when I looked up and saw the burly man with grey hair and glasses standing at the top end of the spur, watching. He was an unfamiliar face on the wing and I guessed correctly that he was a 'new reception'. New arrivals were nearly always brought over from reception during bang-up. I would have acknowledged his presence with a polite nod, except his gaze was fixed on the buffer's rotating head, so I returned my attention to the floor and carried on with the task in hand.

When I looked up again, five minutes later, he was still there, his gaze now accompanied by a frown. Irritated, I stopped the machine and said, 'Looking for a job?'

'Not really,' said my observer without lifting his head. Then, pointing a thick finger at the buffer, he added in his East London twang, 'I was just noticing that you're doin' that wrong. You've got the wrong pad on for a start.'

'Thanks for pointing that out,' I said, irritated further. I switched the machine back on and attempted to ignore him – but he wasn't going away.

'I'm tellin' you,' he said, 'I've got ten certificates for industrial cleanin'. I know what I'm talkin' about.'

When I looked up again, intending to shoot him a scowl, he was looking directly into my face and grinning. 'Got you goin' there, son, didn't I?' he said. That memory still makes me smile.

Cody was a big man then, for a man in his sixties. Not tall, but broad-shouldered, and a solid fourteen stone. After he and I became acquainted, he showed me photos from his army days. By the age of twenty-two, he'd won his sergeant stripes and had had several postings abroad. The images, some of which included army pals, showed a confident young man who looked like he had been poured into his immaculate uniform. In every picture his proud, handsome face was set in an easy smile.

Felix the Gambler knew Cody from earlier years in the system and told me more. 'He was a straight goer when he got out of the army in the sixties,' Felix explained, 'till he had the car accident.' Felix was close to Cody and he said that the older man had suffered head injuries in the accident, and it was from then on that he began getting into trouble with the police. 'Nothing serious,' said Felix, 'but eventually the cops got fed up of him and when the chance came they fitted him up for the big one.'

We hoped for him, me and Felix and Big Rinty. Most people did, once they got to know him. Then last summer he needed emergency surgery and almost didn't make it out of intensive care. We hoped for him even more then. In hospital, Cody lost seven stone. When he returned to the prison, nobody recognized the shuffling, skeletal, stick-aided figure with the wasted face at first. Thankfully, his transfer to an open prison came shortly afterwards, followed by his release on bail. Freedom would aid his recovery, we thought.

Felix told me in a letter last week that Cody had been to visit him. 'He don't look good,' wrote the Gambler. 'I don't think he's got that long left.' This was bitter news to receive. Cody hasn't been cleared yet. The fact that he's out on bail means that the chances are he will be. I only hope he makes it to the Court of Appeal.

17 October 2002

The end of the line for Mickey?

Mickey Folsom was foolish to abscond from this place earlier this year – everybody agreed. How could he do it? After serving twelve years of his twenty in closed prisons he gets a chance to put his life back into some kind of normal order and then throws it away.

Why? In here, there is nobody on his case. There is no violence or paranoia. No intimidation, no threat. So different to the merciless terrain of the closed-prison landings. Nine times out of ten when you make a reasonable request of the authorities here the answer is 'Yes' (as opposed to 'No' in the closed system). Mickey was allowed to work outside and save most of his wages. All he had to do was keep his head down and be patient for a year, two at the most. The parole board would have been impressed with his efforts. Now in his fifties, the last years of his life could have been spent in honest, peaceful freedom.

I know he struggled with the length of time he had to serve. We had engaged in brief conversations when we were both in the same B Category for a while, years before meeting up again here, and he had told me that he didn't think he was going to manage it. Long prison sentences are hard for everybody who has to serve them − that is the point, after all − but those who voice their anxieties are usually struggling more than those who don't. That is why I believed that it had taken heart − and, dare I say it, courage − for Mickey to get through the twelve years he had done to get here.

But one of the big tragedies of long-term imprisonment is the way it can seduce even the steeliest of wills into a state of dependency. No matter how hard you try to guard against it − by planning ahead and being as proactive as the boundaries allow − institutionalization is insidious and unrelenting. It creeps up on you, mocking you while it destroys you, breaking you down and crushing you until it feels like the very marrow is being sucked from your bones.

Yet time anaesthetizes its effect. Years of the same regular routine and repetition can create a warm, comfortable numbness that is difficult to shake off when the end draws near. And that is what I think happened to Mickey Folsom. I think that being in open conditions was too much for him. Despite the precarious nature of the closed system, however draining, however stressful (he hated 'the noise, the screws, the bollocks and the fackin' idiots'), at least he knew where he stood. He was so pleased to see me when I landed here. I was pleased to see him too, of course, but the truth was that our conversations all those years earlier must have lasted less than an hour in total. Looking at it now, almost a year down the line, I can see that what we saw in each other was the familiar, the constant. We understood each other's journey. But that was as much as we had in common.

As soon as Mickey introduced me to his friend Del, I could sense how much he depended on Del's presence. Del also represented the familiar – more so than me, as they had been friends since boyhood. By the time Del got shipped out, I had found my feet and was making my own way as I always had in these places. There was no way I could take Del's place as Mickey's source of support even if he had wanted me to. I wish I had spent more time trying to talk to him before he baled out. But, even though it was obvious that Del's departure had affected him badly, I never really thought he'd sacrifice his place here for a spell on the run. Apart from the long face, there were no clear signs that he was so desperate.

Now his spell on the run is over. Word arrived recently that Mickey was picked up and arrested while preparing to commit a serious crime. He offered little resistance, according to the source. And now in a high-security prison he's awaiting trial. He knows the routine – he knows it well. They say he is looking at a ten stretch at least for the planned 'bit of work'. Because of his record, he might even be looking at life. Either way he's finished. But I have to tell you: though I didn't know him well and it is not my place to judge, I believe I saw potential for good in Mickey Folsom. Now I fear that potential will never be realized.

7 November 2002

'Been anywhere good for your holidays?'

'Stop trying to be perfect!' It was a chastisement delivered regularly by Harvey, my driving instructor, during my first few lessons. 'Don't keep changing down to slow down' was another, usually accompanied by the mantra, 'Gears are for going faster, unless you're going downhill. Brakes are for slowing down.' It took a while for that one to sink in too. Although I'd taught myself to drive when young and had driven often during my years of freedom, I had never taken a test, so all my driving experience had been gained illegally. Consequently I'd acquired many bad motoring habits, which more than eighteen years of imprisonment had still not managed to cure.

Harvey let nothing go. 'You've changed gear, now get both hands back on the wheel! Why are you accelerating so fast? Check your mirrors first, then indicate. Not too close to the car in front.' And so on. Most of my energy during the lessons went into trying to comply with his instructions. But I did enjoy them and I knew I was getting better. When it came to the test I was confident that I was ready. So was Harvey. 'You can do it,' he said. 'Just don't try too hard.'

On the day I must have tried too hard. It was no fault of Harvey's that I failed. In the car afterwards, when the woman examiner gave me the news, I was devastated. I felt I'd let Harvey down. Over the weeks I had sensed that he was not just going through the motions. Whether it had been his initial intention I didn't know, but I felt that he was especially keen to use his skills to help people who were coming out of prison. 'A driving licence increases your choices in life,' he said once when we were chatting, 'and God knows, you lads have got enough going against you already.' The last thing I wanted to do was to let down this open-hearted man.

And what about Mrs B, the vocational training coordinator who had recommended that I be considered for funding for driving lessons in the first place? I had done my best to persuade her that I would need only the minimum number. 'I can drive already. I just need to be legal,' I told her. 'I won't need much of the vocational fund money, I promise.'

How embarrassing when I had to face her after my failure. She was sitting behind her desk in the through-care office. 'Well,' she said, 'what happened?' My poor burning face told all. Then she smiled and said, 'Don't worry, most people fail their driving test first time around.' She arranged almost immediately with Harvey to book another test. He was satisfied that I needed no further lessons save for an hour before the new test. He left his number and I called him from the prison to confirm the date. A month later he was outside the gate waiting.

The examiner this time around was a man. He hardly stopped talking for the forty-odd minutes of the test, making me fend off questions such as, 'Been anywhere good for your holidays this year?' How he made me squirm as I negotiated the traffic lights, the roundabouts and the dual carriageway. When we pulled into the test-centre car park at the end, Harvey was leaning on a wall opposite. He shot me a glum, questioning look, but the examiner had begun filling in paperwork and had said nothing. I pulled a face and shrugged my shoulders.

Eventually the examiner offered me several sheets of the paper he'd been marking. 'There you go young man,' he said. 'That's your application for a full driving licence and this...'

'Er, excuse me,' I said nervously, 'does that mean I've passed?'

'Oh sorry,' he said. 'Yes, yes of course.'

Harvey saw my reaction and ran across the road. I shook his hand so hard he yelped. Back at the jail Mrs B smiled again and whooped, 'Congratulations!' I still glow at the memory.

Despite its destructive power, prison can be a place that teems with opportunities. But without the help and encouragement of good people who are willing to assist and guide prisoners – and, most importantly of all, who believe that prisoners are worth helping – it would be impossible to access most of them. Achieving success in prison – in education, in work-related training, in creative activities – brings personal satisfaction as it would in any other walk of life. But like nowhere else does it depend so much on the goodwill of special people you meet along the way. I'm under no illusions. My driving test pass was as much Harvey's achievement as it was mine – and Mrs B's of course.

21 November 2002

The House of Lords judgment on tariff setting for life-sentenced prisoners

The House of Lords ruling on 25 November 2002 that the setting of jail terms in cases of murder should be left to judges, not home secretaries, brings to an end a long and controversial argument which I and others in a similar position have been following closely since 1994. That was the year that the Home Office was ordered by the High Court to tell life-sentenced prisoners the length of their tariffs (the minimum term to be served to meet the requirements of both retribution and deterrent).

At that time I was in a prison that held about sixty men serving life, out of a total prisoner population of 220. We, the lifers, were mostly in what was officially called the 'second stage' of our sentences. This meant that we were no longer considered to require the highest security conditions. We had demonstrated by our attitude and behaviour that we had made sufficient progress to start moving through the system. For most of us, the next stage would be a medium–security prison where we could be monitored and assessed in a more relaxed environment.

At least that's what we believed. Before the High Court ruling, most people serving life worked out the total number of years they had to serve by educated guesswork. For example, around four years after sentencing a 'local review' would take place, at the end of which the prisoner would be given a date for a first hearing by the parole board. An idea of the minimum term in each case could be ascertained by adding three years to this date for the first parole hearing. The time between the local review taking place and the first hearing by the parole board was known as a 'knock-back'. So, if a lifer received an eight–year knock-back after the first local review, this indicated that the minimum term to be served would be fifteen years.

There were others, however, who had been given recommendations (known on prison landings as a 'rec') in open court by their trial judge. In effect, this meant that the lifer with a rec knew the minimum term to be served. Again, at least that was what people believed. But when the information was released by the Home Office there were a lot of surprises in store.

The High Court ruling in 1994 meant that every life-sentenced prisoner received a letter from the 'tariff unit' of the Home Office. The letter explained precisely who had been involved in the tariff-setting process. First there was the gist of the trial judge's comments and recommendation (whether or not a recommendation had been announced in open court). Then there were the comments and recommendation of the Lord Chief Justice. Finally there was the decision of the home secretary. This was the first time lifers had ever got to see first hand the process by which the length of their imprisonment had been determined.

For some, where the home secretary had agreed with the judiciary, the information made little or no difference. A minority received good news when they discovered that the home secretary had set a lower tariff than that recommended by the judges. But in a high proportion of cases it was revealed that the home secretary had set a tariff significantly higher than that recommended by the judiciary. These were the cases that caused most anxiety.

By the end of that year stories began to circulate of tariffs having been increased by huge amounts. In one case a man discovered that his trial judge and the Lord Chief Justice had recommended fifteen years, but that the home secretary had increased it to thirty. Another, who thought he was being prepared for transfer to Category C as a reward for achieving 'significant progress', found out that the home secretary had decided that he should never be released.

My letter was hand-delivered by the governor responsible for lifers. At the time I was working as an orderly in the prison medical centre. A prison officer escorted me to the main office and I arrived to find the lifer governor waiting, standing. He looked unhappy. 'Sit down,' he said. His serious manner told me it was bad news so I declined his offer. 'I'm fine governor, thanks,' I said. 'What's up?' He handed me the letter and said, 'You know what this is?'

I had been sentenced to life imprisonment ten years earlier. My trial judge had recommended that I serve 'at least fourteen years'. I never thought that meant I would be free fourteen years later. After three or four years, however, when it became apparent that I was benefiting from the experience and 'making progress', I began to think that I might perhaps be considered for release around the fifteen- or sixteen-year mark, hopefully this side of twenty. I was under no illusions about the seriousness of my situation. Life imprisonment was deserved.

I opened the letter and began to read. There were the judge's actual words to the home secretary, ' ...fourteen years'. The Lord Chief Justice however had disagreed; 'In my view a tariff of eighteen years is correct.' Finally the home secretary stated, '... twenty-five years ...'.

It meant, in effect, that I was back where I had started. At my trial the judge had stipluated fourteen years. Now, ten years later, I was beginning another fifteen years. I went back to my cell and sat down to think about the difference in my circumstances. The good thing was that I really had made progress during the preceding ten years and, ironically, had developed sufficiently to be able to cope with such a dramatic change in my situation. But some whose tariffs had been substantially increased committed suicide. Others withdrew and deteriorated. I was one of the fortunate ones and managed to 'stay focused' as they say. Four years later, thanks to a good lawyer the authorities agreed to acknowledge my 'progress' and my tariff was reduced by five years.

Let me say finally, however, that the point of contention was not necessarily that some of the sentences were too long, but that they had been decided long after the trial had finished, in secret, and by a politician. The fact that the law lords have finally put an end to this practice means that in future there will be no more cruel surprises for those sentenced to life. A life sentence, however long that may be, should, like any other prison sentence, only ever be handed down be a judge.

26 November 2002

A last piece of advice for Tank – but not yet

The beginning of a new year can be an odd time for those in long-term prisons. After twelve months of anticipation, counting off the national holidays, noting the passing of the seasons, seeing old faces go and new ones arrive, suddenly it's here. Once the adrenaline produced by the chimes and the screaming and hammering on cell doors at midnight has subsided, and after the handshakes and happy new year wishes have been exchanged on the first day, a lull falls. By the third day people are asking each other, 'Is that it?' Before the end of the first week the atmosphere is gloom-laden as the realization sets in that another year inside beckons.

In the beginning it felt as though each year was a new mountain to climb. December was the highpoint, Christmas the summit. But January was a hellish long way down. Unlike this new year. On 1 January I went jogging with Tank. The big compound was locked because of ice on the path so we ended up doing circuits of the football pitch. Nobody else was out, which left us room to swing our elbows, and the pace was steady enough for us to talk as we cantered. Tank was asking me about earlier years in my sentence. I told him how anti-climactic the beginning of January can feel when seemingly endless years are stretching out ahead. I explained that it takes a while, and no small effort, to get back the positive attitude and to refocus on the optimism and fresh hope that a new year brings, even behind twenty-foot walls.

'But how do you do that exactly?' he said. He wanted to know how I'd managed to do all the years I'd done and 'look so normal at the end of it'. I hoped that that was a compliment. 'But I'm not at the end of it yet,' I said.

Tank has been in three years. If he gets his parole, he'll be out in the spring. He's a giant of a man at six foot four and twenty-one stone, but gentle with it, if a little naive, which is why I never take offence at his slightly over-familiar probing. His questions took me back through a long tunnel. Back to my first weeks in a high-security prison. Doing time is definitely something that has to be learned. And the best way to learn, I discovered, is to look for others who appear to have found the answers.

My first influence, I told Tank, was Dave, the former postman who lived in the cell across the landing from mine. Why certain types of people gravitate towards one another is a mystery, but I used to find myself next to Dave in the meal queue or I'd bump into him on the way to the workshops. A slim, fit man, Dave was always running in the exercise yard or working out in the gym in his 'association' time. One day, as we chatted over a cup of tea, he showed me some photos.

'That's me,' he said. The glum-faced man he indicated, standing at around five foot six next to a red post van, looked like his dangerously overweight and unhappy brother. 'Over sixteen stone,' he said, 'and a chronic asthmatic.'

He explained that coming to prison for life was the best thing that could have happened to him. We had a long talk and later, when I was back in my own cell, the conversation kept coming back to me, especially the part when Dave said, 'I thought: I've been given life, I'm gonna live.' I hadn't realized it until then but these were just the words I needed to hear.

Dave had told me that he decided to look on his sentence as 'an opportunity'. He'd shed six stone and virtually cured his asthma. His new-found sporting activities included captaining the wing football team and regularly running the equivalent of half-marathons around the prison exercise yard, raising thousands of pounds in sponsorship for charity. When I met him he'd done seven years to my one and a bit. We were friends for a year before he moved on to 'progress through the system'. But long after he had gone, when I found myself telling others at the beginning of life terms things such as, 'Use the time, don't let the time use you'; 'Few people get the chance of a life sentence'; 'It's an opportunity – be careful not to waste it', I'd hear my postie pal's voice ringing in my ears.

Not that everybody appreciates 'sound advice' from other cons. But when Tank asks, I tell him – except for one thing. When we finished our twelve laps he asked me what had been the most important thing I'd learned in prison. I didn't tell him. In fact I still haven't. It has been such a hard lesson and taken so long to learn. I couldn't hand it over just like that. But I will eventually, before he leaves. And when I do, this is what I'll say, 'Learn to live where you are, and not where you think you want to be.'

9 January 2003

Acknowledgements

Thank you Joan, Bev, Brian, Roy, Gordon, Ruth, Sue, Graham, Terry T, Vicky, Richard, Ronan, Ian, Emily, Aunt J, Brett, W and C, Rab and Phil and, most of all, thank you M, for showing me another way to live.

> The bird of time has but a little way to fly;
> And Lo! The bird is on the wing.
>
> Omar Khayyam Rubaiyat